*Tea Shop*

in the
YORKSHIRE DALES

Richard Musgrave

- *25 circular walks including traditional tea shops* •

DALESMAN

Dalesman Publishing Company
Stable Courtyard, Broughton Hall,
Skipton, North Yorkshire BD23 3AE

First Edition 1998
Reprinted 2001

Text © Richard Musgrave
Illustrations by Donald Dakeyne
Maps by Jeremy Ashcroft

Cover by Geoff Cowton

A British Library Cataloguing in Publication record
is available for this book

ISBN 1 85568 140 4

Printed by Amadeus Press, Cleckheaton,

Tea Shop Walks

in the
YORKSHIRE DALES

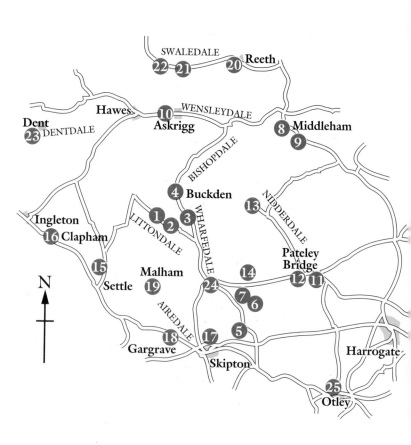

WALKS

INTRODUCTION

Roaming the expanses of the Yorkshire Dales, gathering material for this book, has been a rewarding and pleasurable assignment. Sometimes I've walked alone; sometimes with friends. On one auspicious occasion I was honoured with the company of my youngest son! I've met umpteen knowledgeable tourists, warm-hearted Dalesfolk and well-informed postmen. Additionally I've been blessed in having access to two Yorkshire Dales "aficionados". I remain deeply indebted to each and every one of them.

My constant companion of course has been the weather – the full repertoire, too. The actual leg-work started in April 1997 when Yorkshire was still in the grip of icy climes. Cold, damp conditions remained even as the lowland meadows echoed the seasonal sounds of bleating, white-coated lambs. Haymaking came and the temperature rose but the work had to be done hurriedly, in between showers. I marched on into a summer that everyone had written off – how wrong we all were. The warmer, settled weather had been long overdue but when the sun's rays finally illuminated the Dales they came with a vengeance. One cannot forget the intense heat and humidity during August when temperatures were positively tropical. My final walks were completed in the autumn when the climate was more serene. Fog became a problem and on two occasions much revered outlooks were spoiled. But when the trees and hedgerows are ablaze with their seasonal colours, who can really complain?

Much personal enjoyment has been derived in writing this book – my sincerest desire is that you follow my footsteps to 'discover the dales' yourselves. Happy walking.

J. Richard Musgrave

This book is dedicated to Christine

With grateful thanks to Major F. T. C. Williams of High Fremington, Swaledale

RAIKES COTTAGE

etrace the footsteps of the monks amid superb limestone scenery

TEA SHOP:
Raikes Cottage
Tea Room,
Arncliffe
TEL: 01756
770240
OPEN: 7 Days
– Easter to end
of September
MAP: Outdoor
Leisure Map 10
DISTANCE:
$6^1/2$ miles
(10.4km)
ALLOW: $3^1/2$
hours
PARKING:
Lay-by near tea
rooms

Two walks from the tranquil valley of Littondale are included in this book. This is an invigorating, high altitude walk, involving a physically demanding ascent and a steep descent. The other (Walk 2) is just the opposite, being a gentle, three mile stroll along the valley. Raikes Cottage rests on the outskirts of Littondale's principal village Arncliffe, close to Cowside Beck at the western end of the village. The tea rooms offer sumptuous teas, cakes and pastries which can be enjoyed while relaxing in the colourful, well-tended garden.

Arncliffe's Norman church of St. Oswald was rebuilt in 1796 and further restored around 1840. It has several fascinating features, including a list of local men who fought at Flodden Field in 1513. The churchyard is worth seeing in early spring, when a colourful carpet of snowdrops and aconites is displayed.

From the lay-by close to the tea rooms cross the humpback bridge, noticing the interesting cast iron

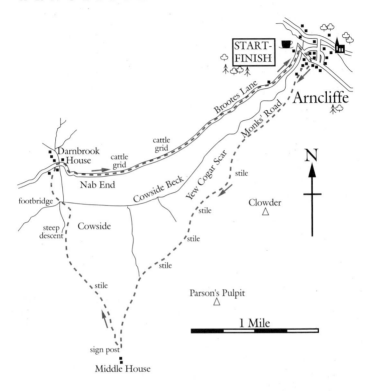

plaque issued by Settle RDC relating to weight restrictions. Walk into the village, but veer right to the lane running alongside The Falcon pub. This lane is such a colourful place during the summer months, when either side of the main track is decorated with wildflowers.

Continue beyond the old house seeking a stile and a footpath sign to Malham (GR 929716). Beyond these the path rises steeply and takes in several other stiles, before levelling out and continuing as a well defined grassy track. The ensuing couple of miles follows an ancient route indicated on OS maps as The Monks' Road, a reference to the monks of Fountains Abbey who had Granges at Malham and a hospice near Litton, two miles up the valley from Arncliffe.

The climb out of Arncliffe presents spectacular views. Also, as the discerning rambler strides out along the Monks' Road, wondrous glimpses of Cowside Beck, wriggling serpent-like, can be admired. Retrospective views provide evidence of glacial erosion in the 'stepped' outlines on the hillsides.

This wild, open, high-level section is to be cherished. It is an easy route, simply follow the green swathe and cross

the stiles until a lonely farmhouse (Middle House), engulfed in a copse of trees, comes into view. Shortly before reaching this, turn right (north) at a signpost marked Darnbrook 1¹/₂m (GR907683).

A clear route weaves through spectacular green scenery richly embroidered with chalk white limestone outcrops. Follow this path until confronted by a wall. At this point cross a stile alongside a locked gate (GR904689) then continue again following a well defined path. Superb walking surrounded by exquisite limestone scenery prevails and continues with views of Darnbrook Farm as the path eventually heads downhill to a footbridge (GR899701). The bridge crosses the infant, yet vibrant, Cowside Beck and leads on to the farm across several fields linked by an open gateway, then a ladder stile resting slightly left of the previous course. A gate leads out of the fields onto a road with Darnbrook Farm prominent. Turn right.

Darnbrook Farm, embracing 2,584 acres of Malham Moor, was acquired by the National Trust in 1995. The farm was purchased at a public auction for £790,000, the National Trust contributing £203,100 made up from legacies and income from the Trust's Yorkshire Moors and Dales Appeal. This amount was supplemented by a grant of £586,900 from the National Heritage Memorial Fund through the Heritage Lottery Fund. A tenant runs Darnbrook as a hill farm with sheep and beef cattle.

The route back to Arncliffe begins with a stiff ascent, then follows the road high above the north side of Cowside Beck. Wonderful views abound throughout and Arncliffe comes into view after about half an hour.

GARRIS HOUSE

Three miles of tranquil walking in the delightful section of Littondale between Hawkswick and Arncliffe

TEA SHOP:
Garris House,
Hawkswick
OPEN: no fixed
arrangement
MAP Outdoor
Leisure Map 10
DISTANCE:
3 miles (4.8km)
ALLOW: 1½
hours
PARKING: lay-
by either end of
village

Littondale was christened by its first inhabitants, the Norse. More recently, several literary celebrities have attached fictitious names to the valley. The lakeland poet Wordsworth named it Amerdale in his poem *The White Doe of Rylstone*. A reminder of this can be found at the confluence of the rivers Wharfe and Skirfare, a location still known as Amerdale Dub. The eminent Victorian author Charles Kingsley is known to have visited Arncliffe while working on his tale *The Water Babies*. Littondale is Kingsley's Vendale. Finally, during the 1970s Yorkshire Television filmed early episodes of their popular 'soap' in and around Arncliffe. Littondale had become Emmerdale!

Hawkswick rests along a quiet backroad, unfurling as a single line of grey, stone cottages on the north side of the river. There are few amenities, except whenever Garris House is open. The village, like its more famous neighbour Arncliffe, is mentioned in the Domesday Book, then referred to as Hocheswic. Evidence of this early occupation is easily confirmed by the 'terraces' cut into the sloping hillsides around the village. Many of Hawkswick's homes are old and some have been conscientiously renovated. Throughout, an air of pride and opulence pervades. One recent conversion is The Ballroom. Dancing to the music of a touring band was a regular event at the former barn.

Leave the village following the road in the direction of Arncliffe. Pass The Ballroom, then cross the footbridge (signpost Arncliffe) and swing immediately right to pick up the riverside trail – eyes down for dipper, oystercatcher and possibly kingfisher! The river is the sparkling Skirfare, Littondale's frequently subterranean watercourse. Eventually the path departs from the river, but is easily followed across several pastures, each linked by stile or gate. On the left of the valley is a towering mass of outcropped limestone known as Blue Scar.

The route briefly rejoins the river then crosses a footbridge and veers to the right of a barn to pass through a gate and swings left towards a narrow stile at the top of the field. Pass through this and the adjoining stile, continuing in the same direction towards a ladder stile. Beyond this head slightly right seeking a signpost close to the wall beneath the large ash, then accompany the boundary wall to a second ladder stile.

Hop over this, then walk upstream close by the river. Soon the path heads up, away from the river and continues through a pleasant meadow to enter Arncliffe close to the former vicarage. Crossing this meadow

Arncliffe's tiny school will be in view. The walk continues beyond the church and crosses the magnificent roadbridge, but a tour of Arncliffe is strongly recommended (see Walk 1 for information).

Resume the walk crossing the bridge, then turn right at the far end following the indication to Kettlewell. The ensuing 200m offers different aspects of the church, bridge and river and shouldn't be rushed. The riverside path leads to a stile and access to the quiet backroad. Turn right.

Roadwalking is often discouraged but this is an exception. This is a delightful road running between

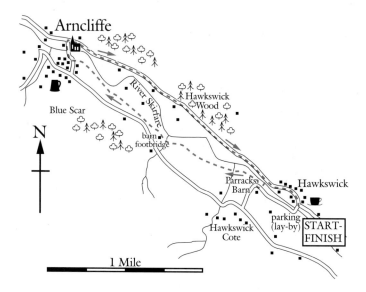

colourful hedgerows, limestone walls, green pastures and high dominating fells. Walking this section also presents uninterrupted views of the more reclusive side of the valley.

Follow the road back to Hawkswick and refreshments when available at Garris House. A treat awaits.

COTTAGE TEA ROOMS

K E T T L E W E L L

A steep ascent offering spectacular views of limestone scenery is followed by a visit to Starbotton

TEA SHOP: Cottage Tea Rooms, Kettlewell
TEL: 01756 760405
OPEN: March-October 7 days. Weekends only in winter
MAP: Outdoor Leisure Map 30
DISTANCE: 6 miles (9.6km)
ALLOW: 3 hours
PARKING: Large car park opposite tea rooms

Kettlewell is a busy tourist centre but formerly housed a farming community. The village once had a busy market each Thursday and was situated at an important junction along the Skipton-Middleham and Richmond coaching road. These days, there's enough tourism to support three public houses, several cafes and a garage.

The village has a fine church, St. Mary's, and a visit is strongly recommended. The present church was built in 1885, replacing an 18th century building which became unsafe and demolished in 1882. Preceding both was a Norman church partially destroyed by the great flood of 1686. The Holdsworth family feature prominently at St. Mary's. The lychgate commemorates George and Mabel Holdsworth's marriage in 1921, and two of the stained glass windows are memorials to their sons, killed in action during the 1939-45 war. The font is the sole survivor of the Norman church and carries a carving of a boar's head, the insignia of the powerful Nevilles.

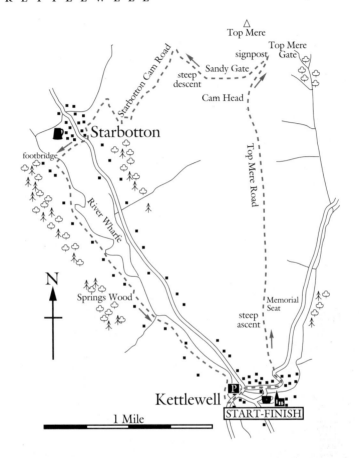

The walk starts from the car park opposite the tea rooms. Turn left, cross the small road bridge and then turn right at the telephone box. Walk along the street to the post office and straight across the junction, signposted to Leyburn. Almost at once the road heads uphill, disclosing the terrain in prospect over the next two and half miles. Leave the road at the second pronounced bend to enter an uneven, enclosed track, Top Mere Road (illustrated on credits of Emmerdale). There's a signpost to Starbotton (GR972725).

Take your time and pause frequently to admire the panoramic views. Quite soon a memorial seat to Eric T. Sagar will be encountered, this can be used to fully appreciate the verdant surroundings. The route continues to rise, although the gradient isn't as severe. Across the valley to the right presides the towering mass of Great Whernside.

Follow the same course until the path levels out and

curves to the right. Turn left at the signpost (GR971753) towards Starbotton. The demanding, uphill section is finished, but the steep descent to Starbotton can be treacherous. So take care.

The uneven track descends steeply between two walls, which have the appearance of having been chewed by a giant stone eater! The dome shaped Buckden Pike appears directly ahead, high above Cam Gill. Beyond an obvious bend seek the memorial stone to May Forman incorporated into the wall on the left. The rooftops of Starbotton soon come into view. During the final section of the descent there are superb views towards the head of Wharfedale.

Emerging into the quiet backwaters of Starbotton turn left passing the Old School House then at the end of the lane swing right to pass in front of the last house, seeking a large gate and a signpost to Kettlewell (GR954747). Walk down the lane, cross the Wharfe by the footbridge and head left to Kettlewell.

According to maps the route to Kettlewell is reasonably straight, but on the ground it twists and turns. It's a well used route, so problems shouldn't arise. One location that does require further instruction is a short distance after crossing the bridge. The key is a stile leading from the river side of the boundary fence into the fields on the opposite side of the fence. Shortly after this spot an open gateway is reached. From there veer right, leaving the river, following a green swathe towards a waymarked gate 150m ahead. The route is now easy to follow back to Kettlewell, and refreshments.

WEST WINDS TEA ROOM

A bridge at the centre of a political scandal, a Norman church, a Quaker burial ground and a Roman Road, make this an interesting circuit

TEA ROOM:
West Winds
Cafe and Teas,
Buckden
TEL: 01756
760883
OPEN: Tues-
Sun, noon-6.00,
Easter to end of
October
MAP: Outdoor
Leisure Map 30
DISTANCE:
6 miles (9.6km)
ALLOW:
3 hours
PARKING:
Large car park
in Buckden

Buckden, which means buck valley, evolved as a centre for hunting used by the Percys of Northumberland.

One of the features in the village is 'Election Bridge', built under dubious circumstances following an election in 1750. Apparently the proprietor of the lead mine situated in Buckden Gill wanted a "more substantial construction" across the Wharfe, to help transport ore to the smelt mill on the lower slopes of Birks Fell. A contender in a parliamentary election diverted monies previously allocated to repair the bridge at Hubberholme in exchange for votes. A local news sheet of the day carried a headline 'There's a bridge in yonder dale and on that bridge there hangs a tale.'

From the large car park turn left, and cross the green, to follow the road towards Hubberholme. Within minutes is 'Election Bridge', a fine three arch construction(GR940773). Just beyond the bridge pass through a stile on the right(Dales Way) then

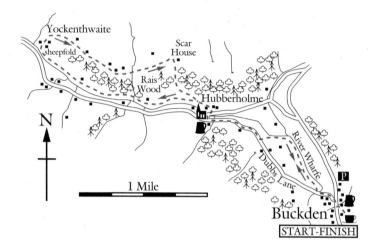

follow the riverside footpath which provides
ornithological and botanical interest. The path emerges
onto a road where a right turn leads to the peaceful
hamlet of Hubberholme (GR927783).

*The George Inn, complete with Victorian post box and
formally the vicarage, stands at one end of the bridge
opposite the Norman church dedicated to St. Michael. The
tiny church contains several interesting features, including
a rood-loft, a memorial to the author J B Priestley and
examples of work by the master craftsman Robert (The
Mouseman) Thompson.*

Pass through the gate alongside the church (signpost Scar
House and Yockenthwaite) and head around the
perimeter of the graveyard. When the path forks follow
the indication to Yockenthwaite and follow the riverside
(Dalesway) footpath for one and half miles to another of

upper Wharfedale's remote hamlets (GR905791).

Enter Yockenthwaite (a Norse name meaning Yoghan's clearing) alongside a sheepfold, then turn right towards a large farmhouse and a signpost (beneath a large tree) to Cray and Hubberholme. Begin the uphill section on a farm road, then after 50m leave this in favour of a grassed track on the left. A signpost confirms the way to Hubberholme. This is the turning point of the outing.

The uphill section is quite demanding but, reaching a small gate on the right, there are wonderful retrospective views. Go through the gate to follow a clear path that passes through delightful examples of outcropped limestone. Another short uphill section leads onto a flat plateau then, after walking through pleasant green surroundings for a third of a mile, the path veers left up a bank, crosses a footbridge (GR917787) and enters Rais Wood.

Beyond this small wood the walker is greeted with an abundance of wildflowers in season. These include Meadow Thistle, Blue Cranesbill, Bistort, Meadowsweet, Eyebright, Scabious and Clover.

After a gated stile turn right (signpost Hubberholme) and pass between a house and a barn. Before embarking on the long descent seek the Quaker burial ground, which lies beyond the gate adjoining the barn. A plaque reveals Friends' Burial Ground – 1650.

The large house was formerly Scar House Farm, rebuilt in 1876. Long before that the building was the home of Quakers John and Ann Tennant, who had been 'convinced' by George Fox during his first visit in 1652. Fox visited Scar House 25 years later to meet the widow

Ann Tennant, for John had died while incarcerated in York Castle for his beliefs. Incorporated into the rebuilt house is a datestone of 1698 bearing the Tennants' initials. The house became the property of the Society of Friends (Quakers) in 1709. In recent years the house has been used as holiday accommodation.

The walk concludes by descending the access road from Scar House to Hubberholme then, after crossing the substantial single arch bridge, retraces earlier footsteps along the road and riverside footpath to Buckden and refreshments at West Winds.

A walk of variety. A wild moorland passage, followed by a woodland and riverside section

TEA ROOM:
Barden Tower
TEL: 01756
720616.
OPEN: March-
October 10.30-
5.00 Wed/Sun,
plus Tues, July,
August,
September and
Bank Holidays
MAP: Outdoor
Leisure Map 10.
DISTANCE:
5½ miles (8.8km)
ALLOW: 2½-3
hours
PARKING:
Roadside
parking near
Barden Bridge.
No dogs allowed
on this walk

The building which houses the tea-rooms was built in the 17th century at the instruction of the indomitable Lady Anne Clifford as a place of worship. The adjoining ruin, Barden Tower, is much older and was formerly a hunting lodge for the same family. The date of construction is unclear, although records reveal the tower was substantially enlarged in 1485. Following a lengthy period of disuse the building was restored by Lady Anne in 1658, but by 1690 it was once more in a ruinous state. The roof was removed in 1774. An ancient inscription confirms the Clifford involvement.

Barden Bridge is a superbly constructed, triple arch crossing of the river Wharfe. A badly eroded inscription at the east end of the bridge reveals 'This bridge was repaired at the charge of the Whole West Riding – 1676.' This work was undertaken following the Great Flood in 1673, when a previous construction was washed away. The bridge was substantially repaired and had new parapets added in 1856.

Begin the walk from the car park at Barden Bridge (GR053574). Cross the bridge then go uphill along the road and turn left at the junction. Before doing so look to the right and observe the old Barden School, complete with bell. The school is still a place of learning under the banner of the Montessori name.

Continue along the road, passing the tea rooms (to be visited later) on the left. The woods to your right are carpeted with bluebells in spring. Follow the road for a short distance, turning right at the first opportunity, signposted Embsay. After 100m turn right again (GR051567) and enter an area known as Barden Moor. There is a stone step stile to the right of the gate.

Barden Fell and Barden Moor are two prominent upland areas, divided by the river Wharfe. They comprise gritstone

rock over which has developed thick peat and acid soils, ideal conditions for heather moorlands and the habitat of the red grouse and many other wild birds.

The area is covered by an Access Agreement which allows the area to be closed to the public at certain times (up to 30 days per annum). Camping is not permitted and dogs are not allowed. Closure usually occurs between August and December. Closure dates can be obtained from the Bolton Abbey Estate office (01756 710227).

A broad track threads its way across the moorland, and this is followed until a wall is encountered a short distance beyond the inlet point of the huge, triangular Lower Barden Reservoir. Ignore the temptation to turn off earlier to cross the reservoir embankment.

If you're lucky, bird sightings will be plentiful. Red grouse, curlew, golden plover and pheasant may be seen, along with raven with their distinguished "cronk, cronk" call.

Turn left just before the wall (GR032571), signposted Halton East, to descend and cross the inlet. The 'no access' signs hereabouts refer to the sides of the reservoir. Once across the inlet turn left again to follow another well defined track to a junction (GR036562) where you should turn right (signposted Halton Height). The tarred surface heads up to Halton Height where superb views compensate your physical efforts. These include Simon's Seat rocks, Lower Barden Reservoir and the green embankment of Upper Barden Reservoir.

Turn left at the road and walk for almost half a mile (800m) to a signpost on the right, indicating B6160 (GR046561). Leave the road and head across a rough,

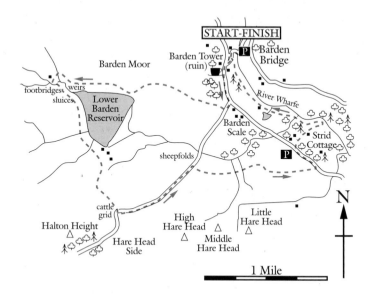

START-FINISH

Barden Tower (ruin)
Barden Moor
Barden Bridge
River Wharfe
footbridges
weirs
sluices
Lower Barden Reservoir
Barden Scale
Strid Cottage
sheepfolds
cattle grid
Halton Height
High Hare Head
Little Hare Head
Hare Head Side
Middle Hare Head

N

1 Mile

open pasture. The path is well defined to begin with, but this clarity soon deteriorates, so take extreme care with navigation.

From a stile go slightly left, making towards the black, gritstone walls 500m ahead. The symmetrically shaped hill to the left is Carncliff Top (449m). The path leads to a wall angle, then continues beyond a solitary hawthorn tree to another wall. Turn right, passing through the uneven terrain with the wall close to your left.

Keep close to the wall with glimpses of Barden Tower and Strid Wood car park, to a large, black, oil container. Just beyond this is an angle in the wall. Follow the wall downhill towards a gate, then turn 90° right, to walk along a clear green track for 50m to a gated stile on the left, leading on to the B6160 road. Turn left along the road for a short distance and enter the Strid Wood car park. (GR059563). Enter the woodland after passing alongside the refreshment hut.

The informative notice board reveals the woods being part of the Bolton Abbey Estate, owned and managed by the trustees of the Chatsworth Settlement. The trust was established by the Duke of Devonshire, whose family have owned the estate since 1748. It is particularly rewarding to pass this way in spring when the woods are alive with birds, including wood warbler, nuthatch, blackcap and many others.

A short distance beyond the refreshment hut leave the main path in favour of a secondary path on the left. To confirm you've got the right spot, a finger post points in the opposite direction to the Strid. This path leads downhill to the river Wharfe. Turn left.

Now follows a wondrous mile along the riverside path to Barden Bridge. Along the way an abundance of wild flowers can be observed – bluebell, wild garlic, wood sorrel, wood anemone, celandine, water avens, marsh marigold, butterbur, dogs mercury etc.

The castellated, stone construction, spanning the river Wharfe, is an aqueduct, part of the ambitious Bradford Waterworks Scheme erected around the turn of the century. The 38-mile pipeline transfers water from the water collecting grounds at the head of Nidderdale to the purification works at Chellow Dene in Bradford.

HOWGILL LODGE

A walk on the green pastures of mid Wharfedale, visiting the limestone splendour of Trollers Gill

TEA SHOP:
Howgill Lodge
Cafe, Howgill
TEL 01756
720655
OPEN: Easter-
end September.
Daily except
Monday.
October-Easter
weekends only.
Closed part of
November.
MAP: Outdoor
Leisure Map 10
DISTANCE:
5¹/₂ miles
(8.8km)
ALLOW: 2¹/₂-3
hours
PARKING:
Lay-by along
Howgill Lane,
100m from tea
room

Howgill is a tiny, well-spread hamlet, nestling beneath the gritstone capped Barden Fell of which Simon's Seat is the high point at 485m (1550 ft).

Howgill Lodge is a well-maintained camping and caravan site which has earned the resident proprietors a prestigious award for continued high standards. Refreshments are provided for ramblers at the site shop, situated off the beaten track along Howgill Lane – use the telephone box as guide when seeking this location.

Start this outing from the lay-by a short distance before Howgill Lodge on Howgill Lane (GR053592). Pass the main site entrance, then the self catering accommodation barn, and soon afterwards turn left through a narrow stile alongside the gate. A signpost indicates Skyreholme – 800m.

Several of Wharfedale's settlements can be identified, as the path leads through the meadows – Howgill with Drebley beyond, Skyreholme, Appletreewick and Burnsall, too.

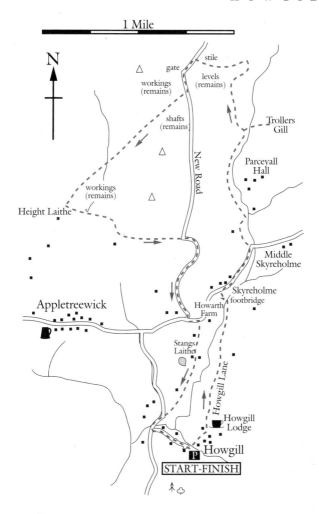

After another gateway is a delightful green sward. Reaching the second large tree, look directly ahead and pick out Parcevall Hall surrounded by colourful trees.

The path heads down towards a ladder stile, then continues across a footbridge. A signpost confirms the way to Skyreholme. Away to your right are the flanks of Barden Fell. The area is known to be the haunt of the buzzard. Look for these gracious birds of prey, gliding on the thermal air flow, high in the sky.

Soon the path travels alongside Fir Beck. Notice the ancient limekiln, in the field to your right, then the highly colourful terraced gardens – rather continental! Cross the footbridge, climb the steps and on emerging from the snicket turn right, to pass through the relatively

unknown village of Skyreholme (GR055604) heading in the direction of Parcevall Hall (not to be visited).

While passing through notice the fine, stone drainage channels in front of the row of mill cottages. Lane House Farm, an ancient building with stone mullion windows and external stone staircase, and the tidy, colourful gardens in the incongruous houses beyond the farm. The last house bears the rather inviting title Banquet House. As you continue along the road Simon's Seat, a collection of black, gritstone rocks towering above the village, cannot be ignored.

A telephone box and a memorial seat stand at the junction (GR058607), where you should turn left. Pass beyond Gill House and a second memorial seat, then immediately before reaching a bridge with white painted railings, turn left through a gate, signposted Gill Heads and New Road.

Continue alongside Skyreholme Beck, flowing between the path and the walled gardens of Parcevall Hall – the latter offers superb displays of early season daffodils. The path is richly decorated with primrose, wild garlic and bluebells in season. Continue past a large barn to a ladder stile. Head to the top of Skyreholme Dam, where spectacular limestone scenery is revealed.

The reservoir formerly fed Skyreholme Mill, which produced corn then cotton, before ending its working life producing paper. The dam was breached in 1899.

The route needs little explanation, but after a stile has been negotiated a short detour is highly recommended (GR068617). A signpost indicates the eventual route, but first veer off to the right and visit Trollers Gill.

The gill is a deep chasm in the limestone rocks, where a vibrant river used to flow. Now the river bed is permanently dry. Hop over the stile to witness this. Even after heavy rain the wet and dry division of the river is apparent. Note the steep sided 'walls' of limestone when looking up the gill, indicating eons of aquatic erosion.

Continue by retracing footsteps to the signpost to begin an uphill section passing through an area which saw mining in years gone by. Light coloured, gravel sized chippings reveal this has been a dressing floor associated with lead mining separation processes. If you pass this way on a sunny day you'll see pieces of quartz and calcite, glinting in the sun. Beyond the mining area the path rises and passes between a gap in the rocks (blasted to give access). Still curling upwards you pass a telegraph pole, then at the next bend leave the main track on the left and follow a narrow path which skirts around a hidden waterfall pouring into unknown depths. (If you miss this manoeuvre don't worry. Keep following the main track. This will deliver you to the same road, where a left turn is required.)

The narrow path leads to a ladder stile and offers glimpses of Great Whernside along the way. This area is the haunt of lapwing, curlew and, occasionally, redshank.

Go over the stile (GR063622), turn left and follow the road for about 100m towards a signpost on the right indicating Hartlington. A gated track unfurls across the exposed, open pasture. Count the gates including the entry point and 250m beyond the fourth gate veer left to a signpost close to a wall angle (GR054612). The signpost indicates Appletreewick and New Road.

The route crosses green pastures, with the wall to your right, and soon arrives at a gated stile in the wall. Simon's Seat rocks should be directly ahead. Cross through the stile then make diagonally left to another stile and follow the indicator to New Road. A faint path threads through the meadow towards another stile at the top, left-hand corner of the field. This is a superb vantage point.

Next pass over the broken wall, continue with the wall to your left to a ladder stile (GR063607) and go onto New Road. Turn right and follow the road for about ³/₄ mile. The disadvantage of road walking is adequately compensated for by the stunning retrospective views of the outward section of the walk. The hedgerows are a quilt of colour in season.

Turn left beyond the (fire-damaged) former Methodist chapel (signposted Parcevall Hall) then soon after turn right to enter and pass through Howarth Farm. Walk in front of the main barn and silo, then turn right towards the camp site. A gated stile 100m beyond a telegraph pole (don't descend to the static caravans) leads through several green meadows, passing to the left side of a large barn (Stangs Laithe) before gradually joining up with the wall to your right and a stile (GR061594) with gate.

Turn left along the road passing the former Howgill Primitive Methodist chapel (1836). Cross the road bridge, then swing left into an unmetalled lane. This leads back to the lay-by in Howgill Lane.

WHARFE VIEW

A walk with something for all tastes. Stunning riverside sections. Lofty, green meadows. A hill climb and a visit to Wharfedale's gem – Appletreewick

TEA SHOP:
Wharfe View
Tea Rooms,
Burnsall
TEL: 01756
720237.
OPEN: All year.
Closed
Thursday and
Friday.
MAP: Outdoor
Leisure Map 10
DISTANCE: 5
miles (8km)
ALLOW: 2-2$^1/_2$
hours
PARKING:
Large car park
nearby

Burnsall is a beautiful spot and one of the most popular locations in Wharfedale. The tidy, picturesque village attracts huge numbers of visitors. All the requirements the visitor might expect are provided – tea shops, public house, adequate car parking, post office, gift shops, toilets etc. The village is overlooked from the south by the imposing Burnsall Fell. This summit attracts many competitors to Burnsall's sports day each year, believed to be the oldest fell race in England.

From the village green cross over the spectacular five-arch bridge. The bridge, renovated in the 19th century, is the fourth construction across the Wharfe since the original was erected in the 13th century.

Pass through the stile (signpost Appletreewick) at the far end of the bridge on the right side (GR034612). Notice the W .R. (West Riding) boundary marker close by. Cross the tarred strip to head towards open pasture, soon

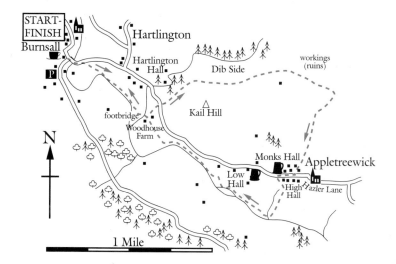

accompanying the river downstream. A feature of the walk, Kail Hill, a green mound, is directly ahead. Initially the path follows the river, with Burnsall Fell always prominent across the valley.

The path parts company with the river, and crosses a footbridge over Barben Beck (to be used on the homeward section). Beyond the footbridge go left, prior to Woodhouse Farm, then along the lane and cross the adjoining road to a gate (GR042607) – signposted New Road.

A climb follows, treading Kail Lane for almost a mile. There are fine views. The imposing Hartlington Hall comes into view and wonderful retrospective views of Burnsall are offered. Pass through a gate situated alongside a barn, then continue to follow the enclosed track until a cross-roads of paths. Continue straight on

towards New Road. Another gate is reached and again
the route is straight ahead, this time towards the wall
corner where a signpost reveals Appletreewick and New
Road (GR054611).

Continue with the wall on your right to cross over a step
stile in the wall. Go diagonally left, then descend the field
following the instructions of the signpost towards
Appletreewick.

Stile spotting is the name of the game during the next
section. Just 50m beyond a broken down wall is another
stile. Then following the instructions on the signpost seek
another signpost on the right, immediately beyond two
mature trees. After another stile head diagonally across

the field to a gate in the bottom corner. From here go straight on with the wall to your left. A gated stile leads to an enclosed lane (GR055604), richly embroidered with primrose and bluebell in spring.

As you enter the lane notice the ancient milepost. Inscribed are directions and distances to Skipton and Pateley Bridge. This overgrown lane was once a highway of some importance.

The lane leads into the quaint village of Appletreewick, a name often abbreviated to Aptrick, emerging alongside the Church of St. John the Baptist and facing the imposing three-storeyed mansion, High Hall, built in 1667 by Thomas Craven. Turn right to enjoy a delightful stroll through the village with its tidy, colourful gardens and ancient lintel datestones. The second of Appletreewick's halls is soon encountered – halfway down the road on the right – Monks Hall, built on the site of a grange of Bolton Priory.

The village also has two public houses and these are seen shortly before Low Hall. Look for the stocks close to the Craven Arms. Low Hall was built in 1658 by Thomas Preston and fully restored by the Proctor family in 1868.

A short distance beyond Low Hall is a signpost on the left indicating the riverside (GR048602). Reaching the river go right – signpost Burnsall. A wondrous mile and a half, mostly along the river, leads back to Burnsall via Woodhouse Farm and the footbridge used earlier. This final section presents a host of colourful wildflowers.

CASTLE KEEP TEA ROOMS

MIDDLEHAM

A ramble steeped in history awaits those eager to explore the fields in and around Middleham

TEA SHOP:
Castle Keep, Tea Rooms,
Middleham
TEL: 01969 623665
OPEN: All year
MAP:
Pathfinder 630
DISTANCE:
5¹/₂ miles
(8.8km)
ALLOW:
3 hours
PARKING:
Various sites in the village

Middleham is famous for two diverse issues. First, the huge castle and the Richard III connection. Second, its associations with the Turf. A visit to this popular Wensleydale village will reveal examples of both. The castle is open to the public (charge), as are many of the horse training stables, by prior arrangement.

The walk starts from the centre of the town, heading up the Coverdale road. Along the way pass the Castle Keep Tea Rooms, resting in the shadow of the castle. Soon after is the Victoria Monument, erected in 1887 to commemorate the Monarch's Golden Jubilee. The metal ring fixed to the ground recalls the time when bull baiting was deemed entertainment. See also the remains of the swine cross nearby. A plaque relates the Richard III connection.

At this point enter a street, designated as a dead end, but before moving on, take note of the moving inscription high on the walls of the tall, black, stone building. This pays

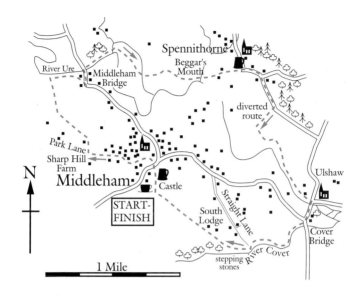

tribute to a former rector of Middleham, Reverend James Alex Birch, and is dated 1869. Continue along the street, passing the modern school and a side street – The Springs (probably a connection here with the nearby Holy Well, named after the martyred St. Alkelda) – to enter the road to Sharp Hill Farm (GR120878).

Immediately beyond the farm turn right, through a waymarked gate to an uneven lane, soon reaching a waymark indicating diagonally left across a field. The large, bustling town of Leyburn is prominent across the valley. Middleham Bridge, soon to be used in crossing the Ure, is also visible.

Pass through a gate and follow a grassed track which veers slightly left, before curving to another gate

41

concealed in the right hand corner of the field. This is often a damp spot. Follow the wall on your right towards a modern, metal gate, with a solitary tree close by (GR115884). Go right and across the field making towards the river. Close to the river leave the field through a gate then turn right to follow a track past the cottages, to the main road (GR119886). Turn left along the busy road, across Middleham Bridge.

Middleham Bridge was built in 1829, a castellated construction designed by Joseph Hanson, inventor of the 'cab'. The house alongside was formerly a toll-house and the Bridge Inn, which closed in 1856.

Pass through the gate on the right and stride across the meadow to a waymarked opening after about 200m. A fine retrospective view of the bridge, with Penhill beyond, is presented. Continue for 50m and cross a tributary stream, then go right towards a waymarked stile set into the wall, 20m to the right of a gate (GR123889). Head diagonally across the large field, following the line of the white poles. At a waymarked gate, hidden in the far corner of the field, follow the directions of the waymarkers to a stile/gate and turn right. Don't be tempted to follow the green lane leading to Harmby. Proceed with a broken wall and trees to your right, over a stile, and climb the bank, veering right. A waymark arrow affixed to a hawthorn bush confirms the route.

Stride out confidently, treading a green swathe with corn fields on the right and a pond known as Beggar's Mouth to the left. Shortly a ford is crossed via a footbridge then the lane is followed without deviation to Spennithorne (GR137887), close to the Old Horn Inn. Along the way you pass the cricket ground, used in several episodes of *All Creatures Great and Small*. Also are glimpses of the salmon coloured Spennithorne Hall and of St. Michael's Church, which holds the Staubenzee family tombs.

At the main road turn right and continue for about 800m to a footpath sign on the right. Leave the road and plunge into a legally diverted way, which has become infested by nettles and prickly thistles. At the other end of this 'wilderness' go over a stile and turn left, following the field edge for several hundred metres to a gate/stile on the left. Pass through this, swing right to accompany the Ure downstream to Ulshaw Bridge (GR145873).

En route is an obvious green mound on which stood a
construction associated with the Romans. Their route
between Catterick and Bainbridge forded the river here.
The earliest evidence of a bridge, probably a wooden
construction, is 1424. The stone bridge was erected between
1673-74, costing £1,000. The tower building near the
bridge is Ulshaw Chapel, the Roman Catholic church of St.
Simon and St. Jude built in 1867-68 by Major Simon
Scrope to replace an inn which had a cock fighting pit. The
cock fighting pit became the family vault.

Cross the bridge, with a sundial dated 1674 standing in
one of the recesses, then proceed to the lane end. Go
right and seek a narrow stile across the road, alongside
the telegraph pole. Next follows a spectacular mile
upstream alongside the tiny river Cover. The departure
point comes after crossing two stiles within 50m of each
other, at some gigantic stepping stones in the river. Turn
90 degrees right and scramble up a grass incline to arrive
at a large tree where you can take in the views across the
valley of Spennithorne and Ulshaw Bridge. Next turn left
crossing a track (rising from the river) and head towards
a waymarked gate, beneath a large tree (GR135868).

Cross the next field and head diagonally right towards a
stile between two trees. After this maintain the same line
to reach a ladder stile at the top corner of the field.

As the stile is climbed the splendour of Middleham Castle
should become apparent. That's the general direction,
towards a gate in the distant left corner of the field. The
gate leads to a lane which should be followed beyond the
castle continuing in a straight line, to emerge in
Middleham, close to the Castle Keep Tea Rooms.

JERVAULX ABBEY

A visit to the lower slopes of Witton Fell, the luxuriant parklands of Wensleydale and the long forgotten hamlet of Low Thorpe

TEA SHOP:
Jervaulx Abbey
TEL: 01677
460391
OPEN: Apr-
Oct, Mon-Fri.
10am-5pm
Weekends
10.00am-
6.00pm, Nov-
Dec noon-
3.30pm
MAP:
Pathfinder 630
DISTANCE:
5$^{1}/_{2}$ miles
(8.8km)
ALLOW: 3
hours
PARKING: At
Tea Rooms

Jervaulx Abbey, built by the Cistercian Order in 1156, is synonymous with Wensleydale cheese. It is generally accepted that the original recipe was perfected by the monks in those far-off days when the cheese was known as Cover Bridge cheese. The monks cultivated large flower and herb gardens and also bred horses. The origin of horse racing connections at nearby Middleham was also down to the monks' influence.

Leave the car park, turn right, and follow the road for a short distance to a junction where you turn right to follow a secondary road known as Newstead Lane (GR 170854). Swing left at the bend to pass Low Newstead Farm, and gradually rise along a section of Stake Bank Road. As the road levels off, turn right at an inconspicuous cross roads (GR165844) making towards Hammer Farm on the unmade Hammer Road (High Newsteads Farm lies in the opposite direction if

45

confirmation of the junction is necessary). As you
approach Hammer Farm, Grey Yaud Plantation is to the
left. This conceals a redundant stone quarry from where
stone used in the construction of Jervaulx Abbey came.
Danby Hall, home of the Scropes, can be seen
prominently across the valley on the right.

The driveway passes to the left of the farmhouse and
buildings (GR155846), and is forsaken on the right,
immediately after the fragile looking barn. Alternatively,
continue along the driveway for 50m and go over a stile
on the right immediately prior to reaching a gate.
Whichever route you follow, make for a gateway resting
in the far (NW) corner of the facing field.

Pass through a narrow swathe bisecting a larch plantation,
then go right, to accompany the boundary towards a
small, metal gate. From the gate continue in the same
direction, with views of Wensleydale unfurling
with every step, until the plantation ends. Turn
left across the field towards a solitary tree. From
the tree turn right and start a brief descent to a
gate. Turn right, as indicated by the waymark
arrow, then follow the boundary to your left
towards Castle Lodge, which houses one of the
moor keepers. The tumbling waters of Deep Gill
Beck are usually audible.

Pass through the confines of Castle Lodge, then
stroll along the narrow lane, past Waterloo
Farm. Here an element of excitement enters the
expedition, in the form of the forgotten hamlet
of Low Thorpe (GR145858).

Low Thorpe has generally been swallowed up by East Witton, although several dwellings remain within the original boundary. The graveyard is on the left of the lane with many headstones remaining legible despite their age. One of these graves is said to contain the body of an infant with two heads. History books reveal another example of human deformity associated with Low Thorpe. This relates the tale of a child being born in 1825, having a hare's head! The church at Low Thorpe was dedicated to St. Martin, and anciently belonged to Jervaulx Abbey. It was taken down in 1809 and its stone used in the construction of the 'new' church which stands several hundred metres to the north, at the eastern end of East Witton. This new church, dedicated to St. John the Evangelist, was endowed by Thomas, Earl of Ailesbury, to commemorate the 50th year of the reign of King George III. It was restored in 1871.

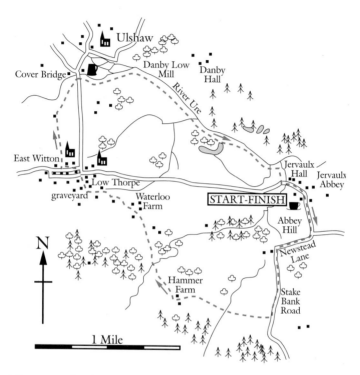

The route leads into East Witton, a typical Wensleydale village with houses either side of a green, formerly used as common grazing land. Immediately attention is focused upon a large glacial boulder on the village green known as the Boulder Stone, and said to weigh three tonnes. It required 18 horses to drag it here in 1859. The site became a focal point of village life as it housed the village's water supply (now condemned!).

Accompany the green to the Wesleyan Methodist Chapel,

built in 1882, (GR 142860) to reach a signpost indicating Cover Bridge. Enter the enclosure, seeking a gated stile at the far left corner. Continue across several additional enclosures, treading the same general line while appreciating long distance glimpses of Penhill far away on the left.

At a ruined barn (signposts) turn right, then left to Cover Bridge which is already in sight (GR144870). Emerging from the fields don't cross the bridge – instead cross the road to a gate. Now follows an enchanting mile and a half, first in the company of the river Cover, then its big brother the Ure. Along the way retrospective views of Witton Fell, East Witton and its church are away to your right. Across the river, there is a closer encounter with Danby Hall.

The riverside saunter ends abruptly at a newly-laid surface. Pass through the gate then follow the track to the main road, where a left turn leads to the tea rooms and refreshments.

A visit to the ruins of Jervaulx Abbey and parkland setting is recommended. The abbey was a Cistercian foundation, dating from 1156.

SYKES HOUSE TEAS

A S K R I G G

A walk full of interest, visiting Askrigg, Bainbridge, Worton and Newbiggin

TEA SHOP:
Sykes House,
Askrigg
TEL: 01969
650535
OPEN: 7 days
Easter-end of
October; some
weekends in
winter
MAP: Outdoor
Leisure map 30
DISTANCE:
5 1/2 miles
(8.8km)
ALLOW: 3
hours
PARKING:
Near church

Askrigg, the fictitious Darrowby in the BBC's adaptation of *All Creatures Great and Small*, makes an ideal location for a splendid walk in the undulating scenery of Upper Wensleydale. The ramble visits four villages and takes in a 15th century fortified manor house, once home to the powerful Metcalfe family.

There are two uphill sections but don't be deterred – what goes up, comes down. These sections give wonderful bird's eye views of Askrigg and the surrounding countryside. In Askrigg note the stepped Market Cross (a familiar sight in Wensleydale villages) and the metal ring used for bull baiting many years ago.

Set out from Sykes House, a beacon of fine fare and hospitality, at the bottom end of the High Street. Go through the churchyard beyond the porch to a narrow stile. Spectacular views of upper Wensleydale's high fells appear, with Wether Fell and Addlebrough most obvious. Continue beyond the cottages to go

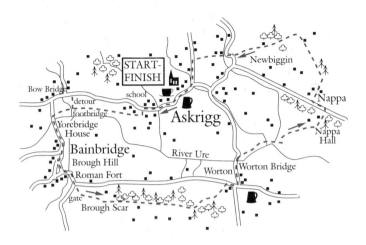

through another stile and head diagonally across the field, treading another feature synonymous with the area, a paved meadow path.

These were laid in Victorian times to enable ladies wearing crinolines to arrive at church safely and with hemlines clean.

At the main road turn right, passing Low Mill Outdoor Centre, to Askrigg Primary School (formerly Yore Bridge Grammar School – 1931). Cross the road to an opening (F.P. signpost) and go over a stile. Turn right to walk alongside the former Wensleydale Railway, seeking the former station building with platform intact.

Following the same line several stiles are crossed before a house comes into view. Pass to the right of this, then cross the footbridge spanning a deep limestone gorge and continue along another paved path. Prior to this you can make a short detour to the right to see two superb bridges.

The farthest away (440m) is a 24 foot single arch known as Bow Bridge. The arch has four ribs, confirming medieval origin. It was probably built by monks from Jervaulx Abbey in the early 13th century as a packhorse bridge. The other bridge is much closer. This is a footbridge, being just 10 inches wide at the ends and twice that in the middle.

At the main road turn left and cross Yore Bridge which spans Wensleydale's primary watercourse, the Ure.

The buildings on the left need to be mentioned. The larger building is the National Park office, but was built in 1850 to house Yore Bridge Grammar School. This school dates from 1601, when the founder Anthony Besson donated two houses in Coney Street, York, to maintain a master. The smaller building, dated 1848, was the headmaster's residence.

Continue along the road to the airy village of Bainbridge. Note the Quaker building on the left just before the junction. Pass through Bainbridge but spend a few minutes on the village green to read the brief history of this delightful place. The next objective should be in sight, the lower ridge on the distant hill, and indicated by a tall mast.

While passing through the village note the pronounced green mound on the left. This was where the Romans built their fort during the 1st century. Bainbridge (Virosidium) was an important garrison during their occupation. The site is private land.

Pass the re-sited Post Office, then swing left to cross over England's shortest river, the Bain (waterfalls hereabouts). The river flows less than two miles from Semerwater to its confluence with the Ure. Continue beyond the garage to a road junction (GR936899). At the junction seek a footpath sign to Cubeck. The route across several fields follows a straight, diagonal line to the top of a dramatic limestone outcrop – Brough Scar (GR938897). The trees show the way. The brief ascent to Brough Scar provides wonderful views.

From the stile go left, following the wall which was obviously constructed by a master craftsman. Note the detail and regimented through-stones!

Continue in the same direction for about 800m until a waymarked path to Worton peels off on the left and descends steeply. This point is reached just prior to a gated stile (GR949897). The path goes downhill passing through wild garlic in early spring. At the bottom continue across the fields, following the signpost indicator to arrive at the exit gate, close to farm buildings. Good views of Askrigg and farther east, Nappa Hall, are seen. Worton village soon comes into view.

Cross the road, bearing right to pass the bus shelter then left into Worton. Note the inscription in the gable end of the large house at the junction. The said Michael Smith is credited with having quarried and carted the stone before building the house in 1729.

Pass the gable end of River View, then descend and recross the Ure at Worton Bridge (GR955903). Follow the road for about 50m then enter the fields (signposted Aysgarth) and tread a delightful riverside footpath to Nappa Mill farm. Along the way the former railway reappears, and a detached white house stands conspicuously on the hillside to the left. This will be visited on the homeward leg.

At the farm walk along the drive but don't cross the bridge. Instead use the stile and cross the field diagonally to a gate at the wall angle close to a telegraph pole. From the gate the path rises across the middle of the field with Nappa Hall increasingly evident. Leave the field, turn left and follow the vehicle track beyond the hall as it rises to join the main road (GR966908). At the junction turn left.

Nappa Hall was built around 1455 as a fortified manor house during the times of the Scottish raiders. The Metcalfe family lived here for hundreds of years, until well into the second part of this century. An inscription on the lead flashings beneath the arch reveals T.M. 1747. Mary, Queen of Scots is reputed to have spent a night there during her incarceration ar nearby Castle Bolton.

Walk along the road for a short distance then turn right (signposted Nappa Scar). Pass 'Brookside' and the renovated Rose Cottage, and continue along the quiet lane as it rises steeply to the previously mentioned detached house (GR963917). This is a wonderful location and Turner the landscape artist thought so, too. A seat has been thoughtfully provided.

Clearly visible are the flat topped Addlebrough, then farther right Wether Fell with the Roman Road running straight as an arrow. That route began at Bainbridge and went almost 30 miles to Ribchester in Lancashire.

Merging with another track bear left, then after 15m take the stile on the left and descend through the copse. There's a signpost – Newbiggin. Leaving the copse the path passes to the right of some buildings, then goes slightly left across the field to a stile alongside a sycamore tree. A clear path leads to the next stile with Newbiggin already in sight. A clear, green path leads to a second stile, then heads right and accompanies the wall to another. From this head diagonally across the field to Newbiggin using the large gate (GR955915).

Pass Willow Garth, then go beyond the tiny green into the lane alongside a large barn. Cross the bridge, then use a stile by a gate a few paces ahead. Head across the field, passing a wall angle, then follow the same line to another stile. Pass through a wide gap in a wall, with Askrigg's rooftops in sight, and tread an obvious route across two more fields. The exit point is a stile beneath the trees. Reaching the road go left, then bear right at the junction soon after, to follow the main road back to Sykes House.

GLASSHOUSES MILL

G L A S S H O U S E S

Woodland, heather-clad moors, open fields and a riverside section. This outing has all the necessary ingredients

TEA SHOP:
Glasshouses
Mill,
Glasshouses
TEL: 01423
711947/711223
OPEN: Wed-
Sun 11.30-4.30
Jan-Easter Sat
and Sun Only
MAP: Explorer
Map 26
DISTANCE: 5
miles (8km)
ALLOW: 2¹/₂-3
hours
PARKING:
Either end of
road bridge

The huge mill complex which subsequently developed at Glasshouses was originally a corn grinding unit. This was in 1812. Later the mill was rented by Thomas and Henry Kirby and used for flax spinning, which continued under various owners until 1972, the final 60 years under the ownership of Frederick Atkinson.

Closer inspection of the mill reveals a number of differing datestones on the building, indicators of the mill's continuous expansion during the first half of the 19th century. At its peak around 1850, 264 workers were employed.

Originally, two waterwheels were used to provide power. One was 16 feet (diameter) by 9¹/₂ feet, the other 13 feet by 9 feet. These were replaced by one huge 120-horsepower wheel. The workings of this wheel can be inspected when visiting the tea rooms after the walk.

Walking away from the village, cross the bridge, turning left then right to

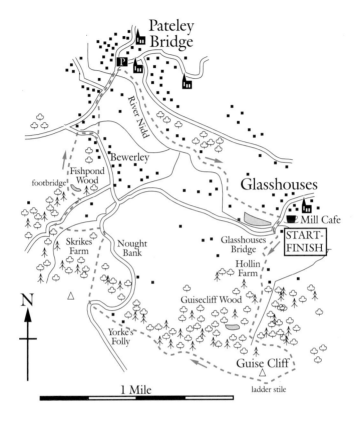

enter a lane in front of some cottages. At the right time of year enjoy the fragrance of the garden honeysuckle as you begin the ascent to the mast already in sight. The lane leads past Hollin Farm (GR170640) and the Bobbin Mill to enter Guisecliff Wood.

Note that waymarking in the wood is non existent and numerous paths will be encountered. Don't be deterred by this. Keep to the 'main' path and maintain an uphill course, aiming towards the mast. Guisecliff Tarn might be observed en route. Two paths within feet of each other pass close to the tarn. Only one offers sight of the tarn.

The woodland section lasts about 20 minutes, emerging at a junction of paths. Select the right hand path, continuing to rise along a well defined route. Fine views along the valley are visible, with the villages Low Laithe, Wilsill and Glasshouses prominent. Looking NW beyond Pateley Bridge the grey/blue waters of Gouthwaite reservoir should be visible on a good day.

Reaching the mast (GR171632) climb the gigantic stile (you're not hallucinating, it really is that size!) and continue straight in front, turning right after 20m to walk around the mast's perimeter fence. Then continue through the shoulder-high bracken, following a clear track that runs the length of Guise Cliff, with wild heather moorland always to your left. Yorke's Folly is the next objective. Along the way are several vantage points and short diversions are recommended to enjoy the views. Take care when doing so.

Yorke's Folly, financed by the Yorke family of nearby Bewerley, was built with a dual purpose: to provide employment for local men at a time when work was scarce, and to erect a landmark which resembled a monastic ruin. Originally there were three columns, but during a wild, stormy night on November 17th, 1893 the largest of these fell to the ground. The folly is also known as Two Stoops. From here the extensive view eastwards includes York Minster, about 30 miles away.

Beyond the folly (GR157636) a clear path leads down towards the road, with Pateley Bridge prominent in the valley. Cross over the road, pass through the gate then head downhill, crossing a stile before entering a wooded section.

Leave the wood at another stile, then keep following the same line down the field (Nought Bank) to a stile to the road. Turn left. After 20m leave the road on the left at the entrance to Skrikes Farm and pass through a waymarked gate. Beyond the gate a well-defined path threads alongside the crystal clear waters of Ravensgill to enter Skrikes Wood, a private woodland reserve with

permitted access. Continue alongside the beck, cross the footbridge and arrive at a road. Turn right. The road gradually rises, then after it levels out and begins to slope down, pass through a wide gate on the left (Moor View Boarding Kennels) and turn immediately right, entering Fishpond Woods which has fine displays of rhododendron in season (GR155645).

A waymarker leads walkers around the western (left) edge of the pond towards a boggy area. If you approach the pond quietly you could see a heron and hundreds of frogs. Cross a small footbridge, turn left and leave the wood at a small gate, then turn right and climb the steps.

Beyond the brow of the hill descend across two fields to emerge onto a road, and swing right towards the cottages (GR155651). Walk towards the hamlet of Bewerley, but turn left at the junction. Continue along the road into Pateley Bridge. Cross the roadbridge in the centre of the town, then turn right and pick up the footpath running alongside the river Nidd. The castellated building beyond the car park was formerly Pateley Bridge station.

The final 1¹/₂ miles to Glasshouses accompanies the river for most of the way, but the last section runs between the mill race and the reservoir. The 650m race cuts a straight line across the inside bend of the Nidd.

Resting between the race and the river is an enormous six acre reservoir known locally as Glasshouses Dam. This was constructed in 1850 and considered costly by sceptics. However, the investment proved wise and ensured continuous production many times over in drought. The reservoir holds 10,000,000 gallons.

BARBARA'S TEA ROOMS

PATELEY BRIDGE

Bustling Pateley Bridge, then in contrast quiet backwaters such as Mosscarr Bottom and Ladies Riggs, all within a couple of hours' steady walking

TEA SHOP: Barbara's Tea Rooms, Pateley Bridge
TEL: 01423 711013
OPEN: 9.30-6.30 all year
MAP: Explorer Map 26
DISTANCE: 4¼ miles (6.8km)
ALLOW: 2-2½ hours
PARKING: Car parks at bottom of High Street

The walk starts from the main car park off the High Street in the busy country town of Pateley Bridge, not mentioned in Domesday but granted a market charter in 1319. There were earlier settlers who left flints and stone relics to confirm occupation long before the hardy Brigantes took seat early in the first century AD.

The Romans quickly established control of the area. They consolidated and expanded primitive lead mining at Greenhow, two miles to the west of Pateley Bridge. During the late 19th century several pigs (ingots) of lead bearing Roman inscriptions were uncovered. One is displayed at The British Museum, London, the other is at Ripley Castle in Nidderdale.

Cross the road bridge then turn right into the park. A signpost to Corn Close (a farm) confirms the way. A busy, well-defined path runs alongside the river Nidd passing a caravan site on the left. A few paces

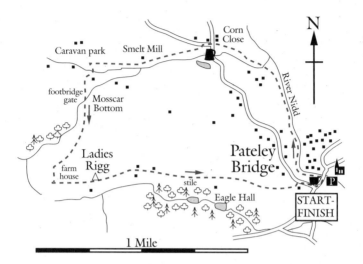

into the second field beyond the caravans leave the riverside, cutting left across the field to pass through a wire gate. Cross the footbridge spanning Foster Beck, then turn left towards the road and Corn Close Farm (GR148665).

Cross the road and enter a secondary lane opposite, signposted Heathfield. Notice the converted mill on the left where the diverted waters of Foster Beck still drive the overshot waterwheel.

Foster Beck Mill, latterly known as the Watermill Inn, opened in 1864 as a triple partnership (Bentley, Eskholme and Shann) spinning heavy yarns. The present wheel was installed in 1904 and is a 30-horsepower wheel measuring 35 feet by 5 feet.

Stride out along the lane for just 50m before bearing left

at a junction, soon entering a massive caravan park. Continue along the road being constantly aware of the incoming and outgoing traffic.

Note the black, stone building on the right. This is the rebuilt Heathfield lead smelting mill, formerly operated by the Yorke family to smelt lead ore excavated from their estates at Appletreewick in Wharfedale and Stonesbeck Down in Nidderdale. The inscription is 'I(J)Y John Yorke, 1855'.

Don't stray from the Tarmac until 200m beyond a turning on the right to Spring House. Locate a NW (Nidderdale Way) sign on the left at the entrance to Low Wood caravan site and pass through the gate. Cross the bridge, turning right on a broad track to a junction. Turn left, entering an enclosed green lane leading to an exquisite spot, Mosscarr Bottom (GR138661), a white painted house.

Cross the footbridge, turn right and pass through the gate. A steady climb ensues, treading a pleasant, green path to emerge onto an access road close to a stone built house. Here turn left along a superb, high level area known as Ladies Riggs. Wonderful views unfurl.

Pass a farm on the right, followed by a summer house then a wooden barn on the left. Keep on the hard surface until a wood is reached. A narrow path bearing off on the left leads to a concealed stile (GR147655). Use the stile then turn right to walk beside the boundary downhill, through the fields. The large buildings on the right are associated with Eagle Hall.

The hall was formerly occupied by the families Taylor and

White. By the marriage in 1698 of Thomas White and Bridget, daughter and heiress of a Richard Taylor MP for East Retford, the whole estate came to the Whites of Wallingwells, Nottinghamshire. The hall took its name from the crest of the White family – an eagle rising with spread wings.

After a succession of owners a Miss Rawson of Nidd Hall acquired the hall in 1870. She modernised it and then passed the hall to the Mountgarrets. Lord Mountgarret had the smaller attendant building erected in 1893. This was

used as a convalescent home "for the benefit of deserving citizens of Bradford". Eagle Hall occupies an elevated south facing site, with extensive views of Guise Cliff and Brimham Rocks. Originally, the hall was surrounded with woodlands and well tended gardens surrounding two lakes. An interesting tale hangs on these lakes, for they have never been known to freeze, even in the severest winters. The reason? The lakes are fed by water emptying from a disused lead mine at a point known as Eagle Level. The level bears an inscribed stone July 13th, 1825.

Continue alongside the boundary to your right down the field. As a barn is approached look across the valley and pick out two walls running parallel up the hillside just to the left of the white houses.

The walls once enclosed the tramway on which large slabs of stone were lowered from Scot Gate Quarry above, to waiting trains at the bottom of the incline.

At the bottom of the field, the unusually shaped roof belongs to the former Pateley Bridge brewery. Then seek the 'faces' on the corner stones of the cottage. At the road turn right, and after a few paces turn left into a narrow ginnel, where a gravestone to the Newbould family rests. At the end of the ginnel turn right for Barbara's Tea Rooms.

DOVENOR HOUSE

MIDDLESMOOR

An outing requiring few route finding skills. Stride out, relax, enjoy the surroundings and the unsurpassed views of Nidderdale from Dovenor House

TEA SHOP: Dovenor House, Middlesmoor
TEL: 01423 755697
OPEN: 7 days a week all year
MAPS: Outdoor Leisure Map 30, Explorer Map 26
DISTANCE: 6 miles (9.6km)
ALLOW: 3¹/₂ hours
PARKING: Small car park at top end of village

Middlesmoor rests on a cultivated plateau 300m above sea level in a vast moorland area. This is the habitat of the red grouse, golden plover, ring ousel and magical upland flute player, the curlew.

The church of St Chad, rebuilt in 1866, is said to be the highest church in Yorkshire... this being altitude not ecclesiastical terminology. Inside is a hammerhead preaching cross dating from the 10th century and also exhibits of locally-quarried Blayshaw marble. The village has retained a public house but the post office has closed

Start this highly scenic, circuitous visit to the head of Nidderdale from the small car park on the right, a short distance beyond the public house. Continue uphill, moving away from the village, for about 150m. Here turn right (GR090744) and go along the uneven track.

The track passes Northside Head Farm, the small How Gill conifer plantation (colourful rhododendrons

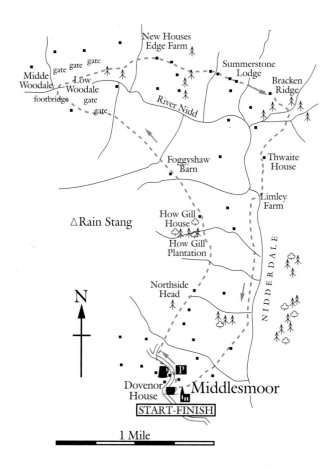

in season), and How Gill House to arrive at a large barn on the left.

This is Foggyshaw Barn (GR092764). Pass between the barn and the wall angle, maintaining the same line as before, to arrive at a wooden gate. Beyond the gate the narrow path goes across the rough, open pasture (New Houses Moss), continuing in the same general direction. There is usually a damp section hereabouts.

Eventually the path heads down to another gate. Pass through the gate, then stride out following a well defined green swathe towards another gate (GR083769).

Pass through the gate, then cross the road (formerly the railway, associated with the reservoir's construction early this century) and enter the confines of Low and Middle Woodale farms. Descend the road to cross the infant river Nidd, prior to reaching the farm buildings.

Continue straight ahead, pass through the gate adjoining
a small barn, then rise up the short incline, through
another gate and across several fields (three more gates).
Leaving the enclosed fields follow a well-defined green
path (ignore the NW sign) and soon a new, wooden gate
is encountered.

*This is an ideal spot to stop and take a view of the journey
so far. The faint track crossing New Houses Moss and a
wonderful perspective of Scar House Reservoir, backed by the
imposing Little Whernside, are impressive sights. Scar
House dam took almost 17 years to build between 1921
and 1937. The average weight of the stones used was three
tonnes, several are reputed to weigh seven tonnes, and all
were lifted by steam cranes with a five-tonne lifting
capacity! The Scar House works were constructed by direct
labour and cost £2,200,000. The reservoir's capacity is a
staggering 2,200,000,000 gallons.*

Beyond the gate little written description is necessary
throughout the next couple of miles. The clear track
passes a succession of remote hill farms – New Houses
Edge, Edge Farm, then Bracken Ridge, where a curving
descent leads between the outbuildings. The clear track
continues, leading the walker to an oasis of unexpected
and unrivalled hospitality and ramblers' relief!

Thwaite House (GR102763) provides excellent facilities
with teas served in the front garden at certain times.
Note the 1742 datestone in the front wall of the house.

The route passes through the garden area, sticking closely
to the wall on the right. This leads to a gate, where a
long, twisting descent towards Limley Farm

(GR101759) begins. To reach the farm keep to the left of a barn, pass through a gate, then cross a dry riverbed. The right of way wriggles between the outbuildings and barns and merges with a road (crossed earlier). Turn left.

Go along the road for almost a mile seeking a signpost to Middlesmoor on the right. From here head diagonally uphill across several fields, each linked by narrow stiles, to a narrow conifer plantation. Pass through the plantation with your destination in sight.

Just two fields remain but beware of the intermediate stile. Pass through the gate at the top of the field to obtain sustenance and those unsurpassed views from Dovenor House. The car park is just three minutes away. Curve right beyond the cafe and pass through the narrow, cobbled streets of Middlesmoor.

STUMP CROSS CAVERNS

A walk by the largest expanse of inland water in Yorkshire, crossing the three main inlets and the embankment

TEA SHOP:
Stump Cross
Caverns Cafe,
B6265 road
TEL: 01756
752780
OPEN: 10.00-
6.00 mid Mar-
mid Nov. Winter,
weekends 11.00-
4.00
MAPS: Outdoor
Leisure Map 10,
Explorer Map 26
– Nidderdale
DISTANCE:
6^1/$_2$ miles
(10.4km)
ALLOW: 3
hours
PARKING:
Nearby lay-bys

Before the Reformation a large cross marked the boundary between the Forest of Knaresborough and the Old Deanery of Craven. This was known as the Craven Cross and it stood near the village of Greenhow. It was removed after the Reformation, although the base or stump remained – hence the name Stump Cross. Nowadays the area is better know for its show caves which are well worth a visit.

This outing can be started from the lay-by close to the cafe or one of the lay-bys at the foot of the hill towards Grassington. At the bottom of the hill on the right a path leads through the car parking space towards a stile and a signpost 'to Grimwith reservoir 1^1/$_4$ miles'. Beyond the stile a well-trodden path goes across the pasture, between obvious limestone outcrops – Nursery Knot and Knot Head (GR082637).

After two ladder stiles follow the waymarkers across open pastures with glimpses of the reservoir soon appearing. The path gradually descends to a stone step stile, from where there is a fine view of the reservoir. Continue to follow the waymarks passing a barn (datestone W.C. 1848) to arrive at the reservoir and turn right (GR072645).

Four miles of exhilarating walking ensue, as the clear path encircles the reservoir, taking in the three inlets – Grimwith Beck, Gate Up Gill and Blea Beck – along the way. Prior to the latter two, and a short distance beyond an obvious ruin, the vehicle track ends and the route continues (through the bracken) as a narrow footpath.

The reservoir is used for sailing and despite this the reservoir attracts large numbers of geese and wildfowl. Notice High Laithe Barn, a listed building, particularly notable for its roofing – the raised cruck with ling (heather) thatch. The reservoir has a capacity of 21,770,000 cubic metres, providing drinking water for Bradford and the grid system. Water is released beneath the embankment and flows into the Wharfe via the Dibb. The reservoir was originally a compensation reservoir, but the increased demands for drinking water saw this change when the reservoir was substantially enlarged in 1983.

After crossing the second large bridge (Blea Gill) the

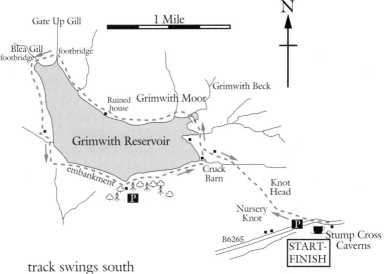

Gate Up Gill

1 Mile

N

Blea Gill
footbridge
footbridge

Grimwith Beck

Ruined
house
Grimwith Moor

Grimwith Reservoir

embankment

Cruck
Barn

Knot
Head

Nursery
Knot

P

Stump Cross
Caverns

B6265

START-
FINISH

track swings south
along the far side of the reservoir,
with Simon's Seat rocks etched across
the skyline ahead. Turn left at a signpost for the
embankment (GR051647) to enter an enclosed lane.
Cross the embankment, an enlargement of the original
1884 construction, then head left towards the car park
(toilets). Immediately before the car park turn left again
and pass the notice board, continuing towards a gate
(GR065641). Fifty metres beyond the gate turn left –
signposted waterside footpath – and continue to
follow the water's edge returning to
the stile used on the outward leg,
signposted Stump Cross. Retrace
earlier footsteps across the open
pastures for refreshment.

YE OLDE NAKED MAN

A magical outward section almost entirely in the company of the vibrant river Ribble. Also visits Stainforth Force and the ancient packhorse bridge

TEA SHOP: Ye Olde Naked Man Cafe, Settle
TEL: 01729 823230
OPEN: Closed some Weds
MAP: Outdoor Leisure Maps 2 & 10
DISTANCE: 5^1/$_2$ miles (8.8km)
ALLOW: 2^1/$_2$ hours
PARKING: Several large car parks in Settle

Settle has been a busy town ever since the Midland Railway drove through their ambitious 'road north' linking London with Glasgow. The 'Long Drag' uphill section between Settle and Ais Gill summit became the scourge of engine firemen. The line to Carlisle has become known as the line that refused to die.

The town, by-passed in the early 1990s, is worth visiting. There are many local and historical attractions, and a bustling market each Tuesday.

From the market square, facing the Naked Man Cafe, turn right to walk down the main street, soon passing beneath the viaduct which carries the famous railway. Cross the road bridge spanning the Ribble, noticing the division of parish boundaries marked in the centre parapet. The weir upstream is pleasing, as is the brief glimpse of Penyghent in the distance.

At the far end of the bridge turn right, signpost Stackhouse (GR816642). A path skirts the sports ground and delivers you to an ancient stile. Pass through this and continue along a clear track, to some stone steps and a gated stile. Several more stiles are encountered prior to joining a minor road. Turn right (GR814652).

Go along the road and enter the prosperous looking hamlet of Stackhouse, to a white painted house – Ribblelands. There turn right (signpost The locks) towards the river, then left to join the riverside path upstream (signpost Stainforth Bridge 1¹/₂).

Across the river is the village of Langcliffe then

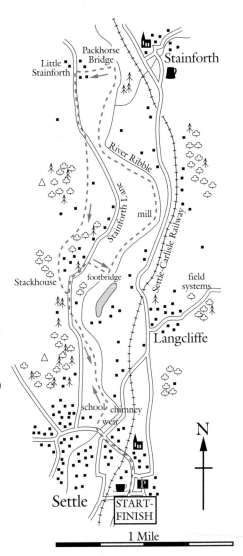

75

soon afterwards a copse is reached. In spring a banking of wild garlic makes an unforgettable sight. Immediately beyond the copse primroses adorn the adjoining hillside.

Do this walk in early spring and you'll never see so many primroses again. In contrast, across the river are signs of industrialisation. Beyond the mill rests the towering mass of Stainforth Scar, an extensive area of exposed limestone. With so much scenery to enjoy there are bound to be distractions, but keep one eye on the river and its birds – dipper, wagtail, sandpiper and, if you're really lucky, a kingfisher.

Continue along the riverside track to the spectacular Stainforth Force and the wonderful single arch Stainforth packhorse bridge, built in 1670. From the bridge turn left up the lane, past the impressive Knights Stainforth Hall, a three storeyed, double gable building built in 1724 on the site of a much older building. Just beyond the hall go left at the junction (GR814672) and follow the road until you reach a ladder stile/signpost on the right. Notice the parish boundary stone (Stainforth-Giggleswick) a few yards previous (GR815666).

Cross the stile then turn left across the field, initially seeking a ladder stile at the facing wall. Another stile follows, then the route goes across the field towards two barns, passing to the left of the right-hand barn (GR815662). Alongside the barn a gate or a stile can be used, then maintaining the same line cross another field to a ladder stile.

As you cross the field notice the pronounced ridges directly above the houses in the valley. These reveal evidence of an early settlement, probably Anglo-Saxon field systems.

A further ladder stile brings you to a conifer plantation. Veer right, following the plantation boundary to join a clear track. Follow the track (left) for just a few paces, then maintaining the previous course, follow the signpost indication to Stainforth Lane. There is lots of wild garlic all the way to the road, which is reached via a stile tucked away on the left (GR814653).

Turn right along the road for 100m then re-enter the fields on the left – signpost Giggleswick. From here retrace your footsteps to Settle.

CAFE ANNE

C L A P H A M

Short distance, but high quality walking and superb scenery

TEA SHOP:
Cafe Anne,
Clapham
TEL:015242
51716
OPEN: Closed
Mons
MAP: Outdoor
Leisure Map 2
DISTANCE:
$3^1/4$ miles
(5.2km)
ALLOW: $1^1/2$
hours
PARKING:
Large car park
in Clapham

Clapham village has become one of the tourist Meccas of the Dales. During the summer thousands arrive, many wishing to explore local places of interest, such as Ingleborough Cave, the Farrer nature trail and Gaping Gill. The village has associations with two famous families – Farrer and Faraday.

The Farrers lived at the principal residence of the village, Ingleborough Hall. They made large bequests to the church and created the lake and woodlands associated with the nature trail. Michael Faraday discovered electricity. His father was employed as a farm hand and lived in the village.

Start the walk from the National Park car park (GR745693), turning right, then left to cross one of Clapham's pretty bridges and then right again to walk along the road. In spring the banks of Clapham Beck are adorned with forget-me-nots, cowslip and wild poppy. Pass another bridge and notice the W.R. (West

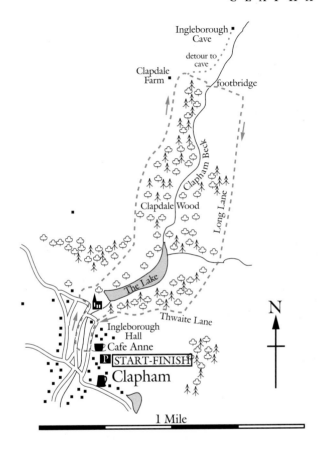

Ingleborough
Cave

detour to
cave

Clapdale
Farm

footbridge

Clapham Beck

Clapdale Wood

Long Lane

The Lake

Thwaite Lane

N

Ingleborough
Hall

Cafe Anne

START-FINISH

Clapham

1 Mile

Riding) boundary marker close by, then the waterfall just prior to heading left where the road bends.

Ignore the signposts to Ingleborough Cave and the Woods trail, instead continue for another 50m to turn right into an uneven lane, signposted Gaping Gill, Ingleborough Cave, Ingleborough. Initially the track rises steeply, then after a short distance it levels out and the surface becomes tarred. First glimpses of the limestone scenery and the woods planted by the Farrer family come into view to your right.

Pass through a gate with railway sleeper stile alongside, then continue beyond a second gate at which point views of the return route become visible. Seek a double walled lane across the valley, resting beneath the limestone scars.

Select the left of the two adjacent gates, then make towards and pass between the farm buildings. Beyond the tiny farmyard turn right (GR752708), signposted Ingleborough Cave, to descend steeply along a slippery, uneven path. At the bottom turn sharply right to a footbridge on the left, just before reaching the nature trail woods. Those wishing to extend this walk by visiting Ingleborough Cave can do so by turning left at the bottom of the incline.

Cross the footbridge, noting the colourful wildflowers such as violet, celandine and daisy. Then climb to a stone, step stile in the top left corner of the field. Cross this, turning right. The route now follows the uneven contours of Long Lane for almost a mile to a junction (GR752695). At the junction turn right towards Clapham, via those dark, unevenly surfaced tunnels, built by the Farrers in 1833 as part of extensive alterations to their estate. The church of St. James is on the right as you re-enter the village and warrants a visit.

JACQUES SIMONS

SKIPTON

An outing embracing three types of terrain. The leafy suburbs of Skipton, green rolling Craven countryside and a canalside stroll from Gargrave

TEA SHOP:
Jacques Simons,
Skipton
TEL: 01756
795482
OPEN: 9.00-
4.30, 7 days.
Closed Suns in
winter
MAP: Outdoor
Leisure Map 10
DISTANCE: 10
miles (16km)
ALLOW: $5^1/2$-
$6^1/2$ hours
PARKING:
Several large car
parks in Skipton

Skipton, known as the gateway to the Dales, is busy and an attraction for thousands of visitors throughout the year. Many day trippers stroll around the markets on Wednesdays, Fridays and Saturdays. Others seek the historical sites or cruise the canal in a narrow boat. The castle, with the Clifford family connection, mustn't be missed. The small entrance charge is a bargain.

The walk starts from Victoria Square, off the lower end of the High Street. Make towards the church, passing several impressive buildings and the statue of Sir Matthew Wilson, a former MP for the town. At the war memorial in the middle of the road turn left, signposted Settle, and follow the road as it rises steadily.

After 400m, where the road forks, follow the left branch (Raikes Road) signposted Stirton. A ten minute uphill slog follows, then as the road levels out turn left at a junction, signposted Stirton and Golf Driving Range.

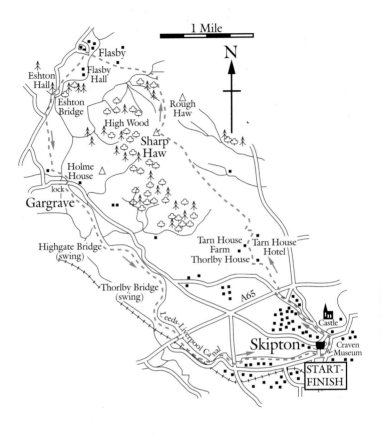

Pass over the busy A65 road then turn abruptly right, following the waymarkers down the embankment to cross a stile. Walk alongside the road and after 100m take the stile on the left to enter a field at a corner. Proceed with the fence to your left, then head diagonally right making towards a boundary angle ahead. Follow the same line to a stile alongside a gate where you turn right.

Almost at once another stile is reached. Cross this, then turn emerging onto the drive of the caravan park (GR977532). Turn right and proceed with caution seeking a metal kissing gate on the left. Pass through the gate then cross the field, between two large trees to a ladder stile in the opposing boundary.

This leads into a narrow lane where you should turn right. The lane goes uphill (ignore the stile to Flasby) and passes the entrance to Tarn House Farm (GR975535). After negotiating four bends leave the lane

on the left to pass through a gate bearing a 'Private Road' sign. A signpost to Flasby confirms the right of way. There are two other gates before leaving the main track on the right. A tilting signpost indicates the route, which follows a green swathe between the scrubby grass.

As the gradual ascent to Sharp Haw gets under way, wonderful panoramas unfurl. Pendle Hill is in the distance to your left. Rylstone Fell, Crookrise Crags and the Matterhorn-shaped Embsay Crag, right. Turning around take in the fine view of the Aire valley and Skipton. Ahead, the pointed summit of Sharp Haw will become obvious and Rough Haw to its right.

There's a sense of achievement on reaching the summit. It's not the highest hill by a long chalk at 357m, but the views are fantastic with Gargrave, the Leeds-Liverpool canal and Eshton Hall prominent far below. If this is your first 'mountain', I hope your fell climbing appetites will have been well and truly whetted.

Beyond the obelisk (GR959552) a clear path veers off on the right, passing through a broken wall before continuing towards a gate resting in a rather damp area. A path leads from the gate and this merges with a more established track between Sharp Haw and Rough Haw. Turn left and start the long descent through the bracken to the hamlet of Flasby, which will be in view. Blue marker posts assist navigation.

The path twists and turns and leads gradually towards the pine forest on the left. Keep alongside the wall to arrive at a gate. Pass through, cross the field (same direction) to reach another gate. This gives access to a lane which is followed downhill towards Flasby (GR947566). At the bottom pass through the gate and in the same direction, between farm buildings.

A few paces beyond these look for the post box on the left and turn left to walk in front of the houses. Just beyond the last house go over a stile on the right (signpost to Gargrave via Eshton Bridge). Climb the steps to a second stile, then walk uphill with the boundary on your left. This leads to another stile. Turn left to the final stile of this section. There is a fine view of the renovated Flasby Hall.

Continue alongside the fence as indicated then, after passing a glorious copper beech tree, the route departs from the parkland, emerging on the road. Turn left, cross Eshton Bridge spanning Eshton Beck (GR941559), then continue along the road (with Eshton Hall prominent on the right) to reach a junction. A few paces beyond the junction find a stile on the left, signposted Holme Bridge.

Set out diagonally across the field aiming to the left of a large tree, pass through a gate then turn right and accompany the boundary to a wobbly stile. Go over this then make half left across the field to a clear cart track. Turn right. Another aspect of Sharp Haw is seen to your left.

The cart track rises and passes some hawthorn bushes. As it begins to descend the outline of Johnson & Johnson's factory comes into view. Veer off the track on the left to a waymarked stile in the corner of the field, alongside a conifer plantation. Immediately afterwards is another stile before a final field is crossed to arrive at the canal. Turn left along the towpath for a short distance then cross the water near the locks, using the footbridge and descend beneath Holme Bridge (GR944545), Bridge No. 172A.

The final section to Skipton takes about 90 minutes. Simply march along the towpath enjoying the rolling countryside and the friendly boat crews you'll undoubtedly encounter. There is an extremely brief section of road work, but this shouldn't present problems. Just keep alongside the water and appreciate the colourful garden nearby. On leaving the canal in Skipton, turn left into the town.

WHITE COTTAGE CAFE

GARGRAVE

Sections of the Pennine Way and the Leeds-Liverpool canal are interspersed with the gentle countryside surrounding Eshton

TEA SHOP:
White Cottage
Cafe, Gargrave
TEL: 01756
748229
OPEN: All year.
Closed Mons
except Bank
Holidays
MAP: Outdoor
Leisure Map 10
DISTANCE:
5¼ miles
(8.4km)
ALLOW:
3 hours
PARKING: Two
free car parks
near cafe

The busy A65 bisects Gargrave and the village is further divided by the Leeds-Liverpool Canal and the River Aire. The Pennine Way passes through as well. Its name means 'a copse within a triangle of land'. The village has always been popular for cyclists and ramblers and those who have dreamed of walking the Pennine Way (but never had the time) can fulfil their ambition in part, for this walk treads the route for a couple of miles.

The walk leaves the town by the lane alongside the larger of the two car parks. Confirmation that you're setting off in the right direction is achieved when you pass Old Hall Fold on the right.

Cross the canal, noticing the signpost to far away places like Blackburn and Liverpool, and continue on the road. Along the way you'll pass the entrances to Gargrave Park, Home Farm and Gargrave House Gardens.

As the road heads upwards seek a

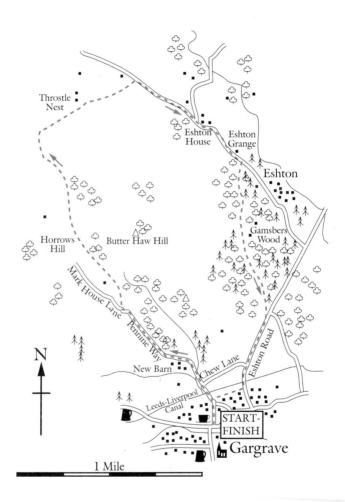

Pennine Way sign on the right, (GR925550) about 400m ahead.

Go over the stile then briefly accompany the boundary to your left before walking across the field towards a large gate. Prior to reaching the gate turn right towards another gate and a Pennine Way signpost beyond.

The sign invites you over another stile then on to an angle of the boundary diagonally right (GR921556). This involves some exertion but good views compensate. The location is Horrows Hill.

From the angle follow the same line towards a gate but don't pass through it – instead continue for a few metres and cross a stile which is followed soon after by another on the left. After this second stile tread a well-worn path diagonally right, towards a wall with a gate in the far corner. From there a Pennine Way sign indicates the route (GR917563), diagonally across the meadow.

Within a minute is another signpost to Throstle Nest. This is the departure point from the Pennine Way (GR916565). As you head across the field towards Throstle Nest Farm, fine views of Cracoe Fell are directly ahead. As the farm comes into view there is a stile to the left of a conifer plantation. Once over the stile accompany the boundary to your right and following the same line, cross three stiles in rapid succession, to join the farm track (the farm is to your left). Continue along the track then on reaching a road turn right (GR925570). Road walking isn't really desirable, but the scenery, with green fields and multicoloured deciduous woodlands, makes it tolerable.

Enter the quiet backwater of Eshton, noticing the splendid Georgian residence, St. Helen's, on the left. Next door is Eshton Hall, then after a short distance Eshton Grange farm, with a 1750 datestone above the circular window.

Fifty metres beyond the farm (GR934563) take the stile across the road on the right, signposted Gargrave. From there make diagonally left to another stile, then cross the enclosure, keeping left of the telegraph pole to a stile midway along the fence.

Now make half right across the final field to a tiny gate in the top left corner. A well-trodden path threads through the wood (Gamsbers Wood) never far from a

substantial fence. Eventually the path heads downhill and emerges via an iron gate into a field. Continue in the same direction towards a rather fine, iron, Victorian stepstile. Gargrave is in sight.

From the stile head between the tall trees, following the same line as before to a gate at the Gargrave end of the field. Continue into the village and as you approach the canal bridge, notice the mill opposite. This once processed calamine which had been mined on Malham Moor. The final section follows the canal towpath for a short way to the next bridge upstream. At this point turn left for a well earned cuppa.

MALHAM CAFE

The attractions of Malham are numerous. This walk takes in Janet's Foss, the Weets Cross, Hanlith, and Aire Head, where the Aire resumes its journey

TEA SHOP: Malham Cafe, Malham
TEL: 01729 830348
OPEN: Closed Thurs. Open weekends only in winter
MAP: Outdoor Leisure Map 10. Stile Maps, Malhamdale
DISTANCE: 6 miles (9.6km)
ALLOW: 3 hours
PARKING: Pay and display in Malham

Malham has long been a popular centre for the rambler, visitor and geologist alike. The village holds many attractions and its popularity never wanes. Malham is always busy. If you don't like crowds then visit Malham midweek in winter.

In addition to the spectacular limestone scenery, Malham has much historical interest, being situated at the boundary of two huge monastic estates – Bolton and Fountains. Another significant boundary is the line of the Mid-Craven Fault, which draws a definite line between the limestone and gritstone areas. This is clear from Weets Cross visited during this walk.

Start from the large National Park car park and turn left towards the village. On reaching Sparth House Hotel (GR901628) cross the road and use the 'clapper' bridge alongside the blacksmith's forge to cross Malham Beck – this isn't the infant river Aire.

That watercourse is travelling in a

93

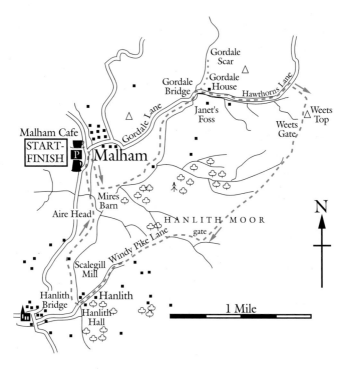

subterranean world at this point, emerging about 1¹/₂ miles downstream at a point known as Aire Head – a spot to be visited later in the walk during the return to Malham.

Once over the beck turn right following the indication to Janet's Foss, a spectacular waterfall. The route is straightforward, but don't miss the left turn at the first set of double gates. The route continues beyond Mires Barn (GR903624) and accompanies Gordale Beck, a sparkling watercourse through a serene woodland section with dozens of colourful wildflowers in season, to Janet's Foss.

A notice board reveals Janet was a fairy queen who lived in a cave behind the waterfall and that sheep were washed in the pool beneath the fall. Foss is a Scandinavian name for (water) fall or force. Another interesting point relates to the Tuffa Screen which has evolved as a result of dissolved limestone being redeposited on mosses growing on the lip of the waterfall. This woodland was acquired by the National Trust in 1982, being part of the Malham Tarn Estate which covers an area of 4,200 acres.

Climb the rocky path to the left of the waterfall, then turn right along the road in the direction of Gordale Scar, a well known landmark and a location that's well worth seeing. A short deviation would take 30 minutes.

Whether you visit Gordale Scar or not, the walk continues along the steadily rising road, Hawthorns Lane. Superb retrospective views are visible along the way, and although it isn't blatantly apparent you're walking along the line of the Mid-Craven Fault. This geological phenomenon is more obvious when viewed from the next point of interest, the ancient Weets Cross, at Weets Top (GR925632).

This is reached after entering an enclosed lane on the right, signposted Calton. As the lane bends right ignore the indication to Park House, and maintain the uphill course with the base of the Weets Cross already in sight. A reward for the physical effort awaits.

The Weets Cross marked the boundaries of several towns which formed the parish of Kirkby Malhamdale, in monastic times and later. The hill on which the cross stands is a gritstone mound (look at the stone used for the walls), but barely a mile away Gordale and beyond is limestone. Between lies the Mid-Craven Fault and this is the reason for the contrasting rock scenery.

A long, enjoyable descent to Hanlith begins after passing through the gate and following the indication to Calton. After about 10 minutes a signpost is reached. Bear right following the indication to Hanlith. Go over the stile then follow the marker posts downhill across the open pasture to a gate (GR914?60).

Pass through the gate to an enclosed track noticing superb views of Malham and the Cove. Seek the wonderfully ornate lamps attached to the first building in the hamlet of Hanlith. There are glimpses of Kirkby Malham church (Oliver Cromwell signed the parish register twice in 1655). Continue

along the road to the little bridge spanning the Aire.

Before the bridge is reached notice the shrine to St. Francis of Assisi in the gable of Badger Hill on the right. Hanlith Hall stands opposite. This was formerly the home of the Serjeantsons, and has been rebuilt and substantially altered three times – in 1668, 1892 and again in 1912 when the front which looks much older was added. Throughout these alterations the original doorway, inscribed R.S. (Robert Serjeantson) 1668, has remained untouched.

Cross the bridge (GR900612) and turn immediately right, signposted Malham. The final mile is easy to follow but there are several points of interest which shouldn't be missed. These are the restored mill (Scalegill) and Aire Head, the point where the river Aire re-emerges and resumes its journey.

Scalegill Mill dates from 1795 and was a cotton spinning mill. Water from the infant Aire was harnessed for power. The waterwheel was deemed obsolete and removed in 1924, being replaced by water driven turbines. These remained until the mill closed in 1991. The buildings were then converted and provide luxurious holiday accommodation.

The route bears left at the mill (signpost Malham) and passes alongside and to the rear of the buildings. Aire Head, the final attraction of this outing, is about 800m beyond the mill, at a point close to the footpath where water issues from the ground (GR902622).

The walk finishes close to Malham Methodist Chapel (1865), a short distance from the car park.

THE COPPER KETTLE

REETH

Lots of waterside walking. We follow Arkle Beck, then the delectable Cogden Gill, before the river Swale is encountered

TEA SHOP:
The Copper
Kettle, Reeth
TEL: 01748
884748
OPEN: Mar-
Oct, 7 days
MAP: Outdoor
Leisure Map 30
DISTANCE: 5
miles (8km)
ALLOW: 2½
hours
PARKING:
Around village
green

The busy, spacious village of Reeth has become a tourist attraction in recent years, but things were much different a century ago. Then, the emphasis was on industry in the form of lead mining. Several examples of the old industry can be found in and around the village – ruined buildings, mine entrances, dressing floors and spoil heaps.

The walk starts from the cobbled area in front of the King's Arms, leaving the village via Reeth Bridge (GR042992). A far more pleasurable way of reaching the bridge is to walk in front of the Burgoyne Hotel (the prominent building at the northern edge of the green), then to follow the lane downhill to Arkle Beck. From there follow the beckside path to emerge underneath the bridge. While under the arch seek the masons' marks cut into the stones.

Follow the narrow path beyond the arch to the road, where a right turn will lead across the bridge. Keep to the right, then after about 150m –

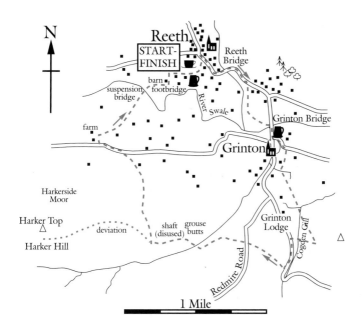

there's a plain wooden seat – leave the footpath via a gate to follow a path alongside the gurgling waters of Arkle Beck. Watch out for dipper and wagtail here. Follow a clear path across the meadows towards Grinton Bridge (GR047986), noticing the different shaped arches.

The left arch is part of the original construction, prior to the bridge being enlarged during the 19th century. Left of the stile are quoits pitches.

Cross over the bridge, then turn left towards Richmond, following the busy road for about 400m. Notice the former Literary Institute (1903) on the left. Leaving Grinton behind depart from the road at a footpath sign on the right (GR048983). Do as the sign requests as you make uphill, keeping close by the wall on your right. There are seven stiles (including the roadside one) and one gate en route to Cogden Gill. The impressive, castellated building directly ahead is Grinton Lodge Youth Hostel – not to be visited on this outing.

That building began as a hunting lodge during the early part of the last century and much later came to the hands of the Charlesworth family. Tragically, both father and son were killed during the last war, resulting in the estate being sold. The building was featured in the film of Charlotte Brontë's Jane Eyre, depicted as Lowood School.

To reach Cogden Gill pass through a wide gate, then proceed as before seeking a stile to the left side of a barn. From there go diagonally left, passing the wall angle to a stile at the far left corner of the field.

Next follow the wall to your left towards another stile, but before reaching it take in the wonderful retrospective view of Reeth and the surrounding hills – Fremington Edge on the right, Calver Hill to the left. Cross the next field, seeking stile number five, then after this pass to the left of a pronounced mound and locate stile number six. Stile seven is easily found by bearing half right across the final enclosure. Watch out for the trip wire!

The right of way crosses and later recrosses the beck without the assistance of footbridges. Because of this, the beck is often impassable. An alternative route has evolved alongside the right-hand upstream bank of beck. Nothing is indicated on OS maps to confirm this. The 'official' route leaves the seventh stile, continuing in a straight line across the beck.

The path then rises diagonally right to a wall. Cross this, maintaining the previous line to arrive at a gate/wall. Here turn right and accompany the wall (to your left) to an angle. Cross the facing wall, descend and recross the beck. Turn left.

In early summer Cogden Gill is richly decorated with an abundance of colourful wildflowers and the temptation to rest awhile shouldn't be resisted.

Whichever route is followed the key to the eventual departure from the beck-side is a superbly constructed

arched tunnel on the left hand bank. This was a drainage point (adit) associated with lead mining.

A few paces beyond the tunnel, swing away from the beck to follow a faint path up the banking to emerge on the Leyburn-Grinton road. Turn left (GR048970). Ten metres before reaching a road sign, leave the road on the right to follow a clear grassed track.

A lone tree confirms the route, and before descending into a depression look over your left shoulder to pick out the recently refurbished buildings of the Grinton Mine. Beyond the depression the path stretches out and soon arrives at the Redmire-Grinton road (GR045973). Cross straight over towards High Harker Hill. Wonderful views of Reeth are visible along this section.

Go along the grass track as far as a recently constructed, sunken grouse butt. Turn right then after joining a primary track wheel left and continue through a gateway and cross a stream – Grovebeck Gill.

The path climbs to a cross-roads (GR033973) where the route turns right, following a wide vehicle track, but those wishing to see the spectacular views from High Harker Hill summit should go straight on, bearing to the right when a signpost is reached at the summit. This highly recommended deviation will take about an hour.

Resuming from the crossroads, the wide track skirts the lower flanks of High Harker Hill, and rewards your efforts by revealing extraordinary views of Swaledale. A patchwork of fields, threaded together by vertical and horizontal walls, ancient 'terraced' field systems, and far below, the suspension bridge to be used later on.

Reaching the road (GR030983) turn left and follow it for about 400m to a signpost – Reeth via swing-bridge. Enter the farmyard and turn right after the cattle grid. Follow the track away from the farm for about 50m towards a gate on the left. Pass through this then go diagonally right across the field, keeping to the left of the telegraph pole. A gated stile is the next objective, from which follow the same line to another. This leads into the final enclosure and the suspension bridge (GR033989).

Cross the bridge and turn right to follow the well-trodden footpath across the fields to Reeth via Quakers Lane. Ignore the signpost just beyond the doctors' surgery, and instead continue along the lane for a short distance, taking the next turn left, then immediately right to enter Reeth via a narrow ginnel.

GHYLLFOOT CAFE

GUNNERSIDE

A scenic ramble along one of Swaledale's forgotten highways, leading to the uplands and a unique historical site

TEA SHOP:
Ghyllfoot Cafe,
Gunnerside
TEL: 01748
886239
OPEN:
10.30am-
5.30pm, Mar-
Oct. Closed Tues
MAP: Outdoor
Leisure Map 30
DISTANCE:
4¾ miles
(7.6km)
ALLOW: 2½
hours
PARKING:
Near bridge

Gunnerside is extremely popular for walkers with a host of exciting paths radiating from the village. These take in the colourful meadows between the village and Muker, three miles to the west, and the old lead mining sites sprinkled along the popular tributary Gunnerside Gill. Neither of these sites are included in this walk as we concentrate on one of Swaledale's forgotten highways.

Start the walk from the car parking area in the centre of the village and head out along the road towards Muker and Kirkby Stephen. Pass the imposing Wesleyan Methodist Chapel (1866) and the cottage named 'Brooklyn'. The often turbulent rivulet on the left is Gunnerside Beck, an industrialised watercourse during the last century's lead mining era. The beck pours into the river Swale a short distance downstream, close to the road bridge.

Cross the bridge and continue roadwalking uphill beyond the bend,

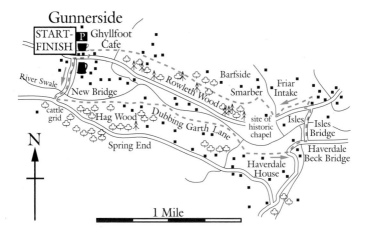

turning left where a signpost indicates Crackpot and Summer Lodge (GR949977). Cross over the cattle grid, then veer left towards a gate and a signpost – Grinton. This is the 'forgotten highway' – Dubbing Garth Lane. A wondrous couple of miles are about to unfold, revealing an array of colourful wildflowers as the lane threads along the valley, never far from the rumbustious river Swale.

After 800m a glimpse of Gunnerside village appears in the gaps between the trees. Soon afterwards the river curves north, briefly parting from the close company of the lane. When the river renews the relationship, look across to the green mass of Rowleth Wood to be seen at close quarters later on.

Keep striding along the lane to a junction just beyond a delightful farm cottage, Dubbing Garth. Dubb is Old English for 'pool' and 'Garth' Norse for enclosure. At the

point where the lane meets with a metalled road (GR
976972) turn left, then left again (signposted Reeth and
Richmond) to cross Isles Bridge. Walk along the road,
passing the row of cottages to the main road. Turn left,
and walk along the main road for a short way to the
boundary of Low Row. Immediately beyond the
boundary sign turn right, and begin the ascent of a
grassed incline which soon becomes tree covered.

Emerging from the trees out on to open pasture, turn left

(GR978976) to walk above the tree line on your left. Continue in the same line, passing through two gates then, having negotiated an often damp area, make towards a large barn (sometimes referred to as cow houses in Swaledale).

Adjoining the barn is the unique historical site. A newly installed gate leads to the site of the first Independent Church in Swaledale, founded by Philip, Lord Wharton, in 1690. A solitary tombstone reveals details of the Brown family, who lived at Barfside (800m north). John Brown died in 1868, aged 74. Mary Brown died in 1870, aged 76, and their daughter Elizabeth died in 1874, aged 40.

Resume the walk passing through the gate alongside the barn then make towards Smarber Farm (GR974977), tackling the steep incline directly ahead, then a gate to a second field. As the farm is approached turn 90 degrees left, to follow the boundary to a gate close to the wall corner.

Maintain a westerly course to a gated stile slotted into the facing wall. There are three more walls each with obvious exits before entering the delightful Rowleth Wood (GR968977). A well worn path maintains an almost unwavering course through the wood but should doubt arise, the rule is ascend in preference to descend.

Emerging from the wood into a clearing superb views of Swaledale are presented. Maintain the same course as before to a stile on the left of some large trees. Another stile to the right of the second telegraph pole cannot be missed, as you cross these upland enclosures.

Note the large number of field barns, one of Swaledale's

characteristics. Also, far below there are retrospective glimpses of Dubbing Garth Lane and the twin arches of Gunnerside Bridge.

Several other stiles are negotiated before emerging on to an obvious green track (GR959983), which heads steeply downhill. This magnificent descent affords wonderful views as it leads the satisfied traveller back to Gunnerside and refreshment at Ghyllfoot.

OLD SCHOOL TEA ROOMS

An outing covering both sides of the valley, centred on the villages of Muker and Thwaite which have Scandinavian origins, meaning cultivated field and a clearing

TEA SHOP:
The Old School
Tea Rooms,
Muker
TEL: 01748
886337
OPEN: Easter-
end Oct. Closed
Mons, except
Bank Hols
MAP: Outdoor
Leisure Map 30
DISTANCE: 4
miles
ALLOW: 2
hours
PARKING
Large car park
in village

Muker lies towards the western end of Swaledale, nestling beneath Kisdon Hill (499m). A quiet outpost, yet inhabited throughout the year. The village has amenities often associated with larger, more accessible locations: pub, post office, tea rooms, toilets, car park and a village hall. Muker has one other attraction – a wonderful village band. Muker Silver Band was founded in 1897.

The church of St. Mary was built in 1580 as a chapel of ease to St. Andrew's, Grinton, 10 miles east. Before that date, those needing a Christian burial were carried manually to Grinton in wicker coffins following a treacherous route known as The Corpse Road. This involved walking 14 miles from Keld, 12 from Thwaite and 10 from Muker. These journeys took two days each way.

Start the walk from the car park near the bridge spanning Straw Beck. Don't cross the bridge. Instead go down the uneven lane on the right, signposted Occupation Road.

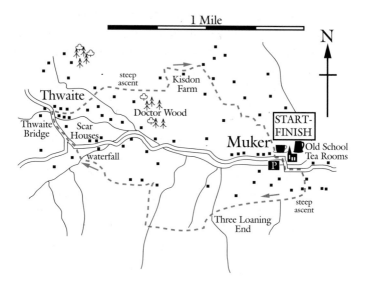

Continue along this track as it rises steadily for almost a mile to a junction indicated on maps as Three Loaning End – three lanes meet – (GR904973). Along the way there are superb views of Muker, Kisdon Hill and the distant Swale Gorge.

Fine displays of wildflowers are witnessed in the spring – primrose, wood anemones, stitchwort, bluebell and in the final 400m before the junction, fragrant orchid as well. Kisdon Hill is symmetrical when viewed from the junction.

At the junction turn right to follow a level, ancient highway, walking at a lofty altitude often in the company of curlew, lapwing and golden plover. About 800m later (GR899973), swing right again to descend another enclosed lane, often decorated by cuckoo flower and marsh marigold, to arrive at a square, upright barn. Here turn left and go through a gate (GR900977). Go straight ahead, crossing a tiny stream to enter another enclosed section. After passing the second barn to your right, there are two gates in quick succession. Pass through these and begin the descent to Thwaite, a collection of grey stone cottages in the valley. The closer hamlet is Scar Houses. As you descend towards a small wooden gate, one of Swaledale's characteristics is visible – the large numbers of field barns.

Cross the tiny footbridge by the waterfalls – there's a larger one downstream – then join a wide track to join the road (GR893980). Turn left into Thwaite, a small village comprising tidy, stone built cottages. Refreshments can be obtained at Kearton Guest House.

Note the Victorian post box, set into the wall opposite the telephone box.

Having entered the village via the small, arched road bridge, turn right at the cafe (GR983892) then go along the road to a signpost beyond Thwaite Farm. The next mile and a half follows the Pennine Way to Kisdon Farm (GR903985).

From the signpost and stile at Thwaite Farm follow the indication 'Pennine Way and Muker' (ignore the turn to Angram). At a junction swing left (Pennine Way) and cross two meadows to reach a gate. Beyond this bear right, then left to follow the field boundary to a narrow stile close to a barn. Go through the stile, turning right as indicated by the Pennine Way sign (GR896984) to begin the ascent of the lower flanks of Kisdon Hill. This section offers superb retrospective views.

Reaching a point where the path swings sharply left and a barn rests below, look across the valley and identify the enclosed lane, descended earlier. From there the path rises to a stile, before levelling out and turning left towards a gate directly ahead. Pass through, making towards Kisdon Farm in view to your right (GR903986).

At the farm go through the adjoining gates and rise towards a junction where you should turn right. Now begins a spectacular descent to Muker (a grand finale). Entering the village turn right at the first junction, then left, to pass the post office, the village hall (1922) and the Literary Institute, en route to refreshments at the Old School, resting immediately beyond Swaledale Woollens.

MEADOWSIDE TEA ROOM

DENT

After an invigorating ascent of Flinter Gill, the rest of this walk is surprisingly easy. Sections beneath Combe Top and along the Dee are particularly rewarding

TEA SHOP:
Meadowside Tea
Room, Dent
TEL: 015396
25329
OPEN: 7 days
in season.
Weekends only
Nov-Easter
MAP: Outdoor
Leisure Map 2
DISTANCE:
6½ miles
(10.4km)
ALLOW: 3½-4
hours
PARKING:
Large car park in
village

Historians will cherish a visit to Dent which contains a wealth of interesting historical information, some of it associated with long forgotten industries such as knitting and marble. The village, with its cobbled streets, has affiliations with the Sedgwick family. A time long past is the mood in Dent, although its tiny brewery and tourism are modern industries and add to the character and resilience of the town.

Begin the walk from the main car park (GR704871), cross the road and enter the lane to the left of the 'National School' building. A plaque shows the school was built in 1845. Continue past the village green towards Flinter Gill, a signpost confirming the way.

The road heads ominously uphill and passes the Zion Chapel (1835), then beyond the appropriately named Ghyll Head Cottage the surface deteriorates, adding to breathing problems! However, it isn't all bad news. Flinter Gill is a spectacular

113

ravine, concealing a succession of waterfalls, the banks of which are bedecked with an array of colourful wildflowers in season.

The hard work lasts for about 35 minutes, ending at a junction with a broad, enclosed track known as Occupation Road. The name was acquired around 1860, when numerous upland fells were being enclosed or 'occupied' (GR698858).

Close to the junction you'll see (and probably use) a memorial seat, donated by the friends of John H. McNeil.

From the junction turn right, signposted Keldishaw. There follows a bracing, high level tramp along an ancient highway which once linked Ingleton and Lancaster. As this wonderful section unfolds, the unmistakable mass of Middleton Fell seems to increase in stature. There are also fine views of the Howgill Fells.

Reaching the end of the 'Occy' (GR679862) turn right to tread the road for 400m to a gate on the left, signposted Underwood. A clear, green path leads to a ladder stile over the wall to your left. Cross this, then head towards the path which skirts the lower flanks of the hill directly ahead. To reach this path you may encounter a brief boggy section.

The hillside path curves right and quickly develops into a pleasant green sward. Excellent views of Dentdale are presented (GR683871). Go around the derelict farm (Combe House), continuing downhill from the rear of the building and walking alongside the scant remains of a wall. The track becomes clearer and soon passes through an opening in a wall after which you should turn right.

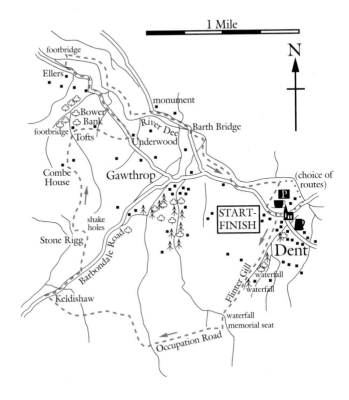

The immediate objective is Tofts Farm, already in sight (GR683878). The prominent mound of Helms Knott rests across the valley.

To reach the farm use a tiny stone footbridge, concealed in a depression and found by bearing left towards a large tree. Leave the farmyard by the facing gate, then descend along the drive towards the road and Underwood farm, passing the refurbished Bower Bank en-route. At the road (GR688877) turn left and follow it to Ellers footbridge, ignoring the temptation to visit Dallicar farm along the way.

Cross the footbridge (GR679886) then turn right, signposted Monument. A fine 1000m alongside the river Dee ensues, and there may be sightings of dipper or kingfisher. The riverside path eventually rises and leads to a road where you turn right. The monument is opposite.

The inscription reads: 'This stone was erected by the landowners and inhabitants of Dent in grateful acknowledgement to Lucy Elam at whose sole charge this deviation road 1,122 yards in length was made in 1876. In filial love and remembrance and to fulfil the wishes of her father John Elam.'

Continue along the roadside to cross Barth Bridge (GR695879), then turn left

through a stile. Several colourful meadows are crossed before a short road section. The riverside path soon resumes on the left, and eventually a choice of routes into Dent is offered.

Those wishing to make directly to the tea shop should turn 90 degrees right when the opportunity presents itself – seeing the cars in the car park is the main clue. Follow this route to the angle in the right hand corner of a field, where you'll find a stile. Pass through the stile, then turn left – after you join the road the tea shop is to the right.

The slightly longer route, taking in St. Andrew's church and the oldest parts of the village, continues along the riverside to Church Bridge, where a right turn leads into the churchyard and the historical attractions to be found in the village.

CRACOE CAFE

C R A C O E

An outing to the green, open pastures of Craven. The highlight is a visit to Linton in Craven, one Yorkshire's prettiest spots

TEA SHOP:
Cracoe Cafe,
Cracoe
TEL: 01756
730228
OPEN: 7 days
10.30am-
6.30pm. Winter
weekdays
10.30am-
5.30pm
DISTANCE:
5¹/₂ miles
(8.8km)
ALLOW: 2¹/₂-3
hours
MAP: Outdoor
Leisure Map 10
PARKING: Lay-
by 400m west of
village

Cracoe is on the busy B6265 Skipton-Grassington road. It is a tidy village, comprising a mixture of old and modern dwellings and several working farms. The village is overlooked by the imposing Cracoe Fell on which stands the 35 foot high obelisk, the Great War Monument known locally as Cracoe Pinnacle. Those ascending the fell will be rewarded by views which can extend to the Cumbrian fells. The outing which follows doesn't visit the monument, but has other attractions – spectacular rolling, countryside and a visit to Linton in Craven.

Parking at Cracoe Cafe is limited and reserved for clients. Walkers are asked to use the large lay-by at the Skipton side of the village and not the public house car park.

From the lay-by follow the road (footpath on one side) through the village, towards the chevron road sign where the road bends. As you approach this look left across the

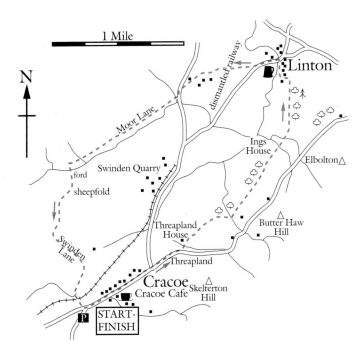

fields and pinpoint a large barn which will be encountered towards the end of this outing.

On reaching the bend (GR982604) leave the main road to go down a secondary road opposite. Walk along this road for 200m, then bear left where it splits, signposted Linton. Walk towards Threapland Farm, but turn right immediately before the farmhouse and pass through a metal gate (there's a signpost almost concealed by the horse chestnut tree). Go beyond the barn, pass through another gate, then walk along an enclosed section which ends soon after, close to a ramshackle sheepfold.

Continue across the field following a well defined track,
adjacent to the unsightly Swinden Quarry. At an open
gateway bear diagonally right, towards the fence angle in
view across the field. Notice the ancient limekiln nearby.
Walk alongside the fence to a ladder stile beneath the trees.

From the stile the route maintains the same general
course across ten fields, en route to Linton in Craven.
Open gateways guide through the first two fields, then
after entering the third, bear half left seeking a ladder
stile towards the lower left-hand corner. After this, cross
two narrow fields, then a wider one, and pass through a
stile to the left side of a barn (GR998618). The
farmhouse nearby is Ings House.

Beyond the barn go through a gateway, then bear slightly right seeking a stone step stile in a recently repaired wall. Continue alongside the wall on the right, with the dome-shaped almshouses at Linton in view. At a wide gate use the wooden side gate, then continue up a brief incline to merge with an obvious farm track, bearing left towards a gate. This track is followed and leads to the picturesque village of Linton in Craven. The deciduous woodland on the right is Brows Plantation.

Entering the village one is instantly impressed by numerous examples of local pride. Tidy, well maintained cottages and colourful gardens abound. The village has an inn and many 17th and 18th century dwellings, all south facing, and most have lintel datestones. The astrolabe on the green commemorates the village winning a 'Best Kept Village' competition in 1949.

Linton Beck, unsullied and usually soundless, divides the village. It has five crossing points during its brief journey through the village. The road bridge, built in 1892; packhorse bridge, restored 17th century; clapper (foot) bridge; stepping stones and ford. One notable omission is a church: that's alongside the river Wharfe almost 800m away. There is, however, a place of worship in the almshouses at the southern end of the green. This grand, Palladian style building was designed by Sir John Vanbrugh, and built of Ashlar blocks of millstone grit, taken from Thorpe Fell quarries, nearby.

The almshouses were provided by Linton's 'Dick Whittington' – Richard Fountaine. He was born there in 1640 and departed as a young man, never to return. Fountaine made his fortune in London as a timber merchant, at a time when

*timber was in great demand following the plague of 1665
and the Great Fire, a year later.*

*Fountaine died aged 81, a wealthy man, but never forgot
his upbringing and his home village. He left monies for a
hospital (almshouses). Details of his complex will can be
obtained from the informative sheets on sale at the chapel
within the almshouses.*

Resume the walk from the almshouses then pass beyond
the inn and turn left at the junction. The building
encountered is Old Hall, the oldest portions dating from
the 17th century. Continue along the road for 250m before
turning right and entering a lane signposted Cracoe
(GR994627). Several hundred metres along the lane is a
stone bridge. It crossed the disused Skipton-Grassington
railway, once a well-used branch line. From here there are
fine views of Cracoe Fell and the obelisk. Also, three
dome-shaped hills in front of Cracoe Fell are apparent.

*These are drumlins, sometimes called reef knolls, large
mounds of pure limestone deposited by glacial movement
thousands of years ago. Left to right, they are Elbolton Hill,
Butter Haw Hill and Skelterton Hill.*

Continue beyond the bridge to an ancient railway
carriage (summer house) on the right. Here the hard,
gravelled surface ends and the way ahead continues in the
same direction, following an enclosed grassy track.
Eventually this goes down and joins the B6265 road. Go
straight across the road to enter another enclosed lane
(Moor Lane, GR985623). A signpost indicates Cracoe
2^1/$_4$ miles.

The lane winds on and little needs to be said except,

perhaps, to point out that the route is now passing to the rear of Swinden Quarry. Eventually a sheepfold is encountered, beyond which the enclosed section ends and the way continues across the rough pasture, in the form of a clear, winding path. Soon, a railway sleeper bridge aids the crossing of a boggy section. At this point start counting the blue tipped marker posts.

Six paces beyond the fourth post, turn left to descend and cross Eller Beck to a gate on the opposite bank (GR972616). Pass through the gate then bear left up a green path with the mature trees to your right. At the wall end turn right, then head half left aiming for a ruined sheepfold which isn't obvious. From the sheepfold accompany the wall uphill, across the thistle infested pasture to pass to the right of the large barn mentioned at the outset. Beyond the barn accompany the wall on the left as far as the angle. From there aim diagonally left across the field to a gate.

Take in the wonderful scenery with Sharp Haw and Rough Haw prominent directly ahead, and the unmistakable flat topped Pendle Hill in the distance.

Pass through the first gate, then select the right hand one of two facing gates. This leads into an enclosed, green lane (Swinden Lane) and is followed slavishly, despite several 90 degree turns, to emerge at the main road. Turn left for Cracoe Cafe or right for the lay-by.

THE DALES CAFE

An ideal outing for short winter days or a summer evening. There are superb views and a visit to the hidden hamlet of Clifton

TEA SHOP:
The Dales Cafe,
Otley
TEL: 01943
850980
OPEN: 7 days
throughout the
year
MAPS: Explorer
Map 27, Stile
Maps Chevin
Area
DISTANCE:
5$\frac{1}{2}$ miles
ALLOW: 2$\frac{1}{2}$
hours
PARKING:
Several large car
parks

Otley is still a bustling market town despite being by-passed several years ago. The town once boasted more public houses per head of population than anywhere else in England – 27! Otley has always supported the farming community, but has had associations with other industries. Thomas Chippendale, the master cabinetmaker, lived in the town, and the engineering company founded by Messrs Dawson, Payne and Elliot produced printing presses installed all over the world. The town centre has some notable buildings, and a leaflet produced by Otley Civic Society pinpoints these in a townwalk.

Wherever you're able to park, make your way to All Saints' parish church, a Norman foundation that has retained the original north door and has fragments of Saxon crosses. The church overlooks Bondgate. Go along the ginnel to the right of the church. A short distance into the ginnel is a splendid memorial to the men who died while building Bramhope Tunnel. Known as the

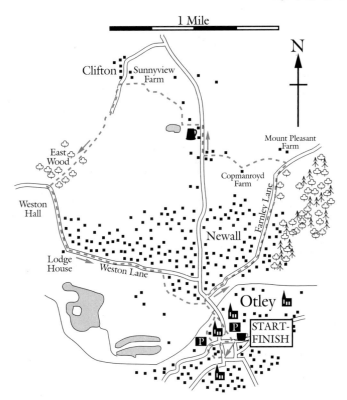

Navvies Monument, it relates details of men who died between 1846-49.

Bramhope Tunnel was cut through rock on the railway between Leeds and Thirsk. It is almost three miles long. A labour force of 2,300 men and 400 horses were involved. The monument is a miniature of the northern portal.

Go along the ginnel to the main road, cross over, turn right then left beyond Lund's and continue through a small park.

Evidence of former grandeur is recorded at the site of the Archbishop's Manor House. A 13th century building once stood here. Leave the park, turn left and cross the seven-arch bridge, then turn right into Farnley Lane. Initially, the terrain is level, but height is gained as the way continues beyond Prince Henry's Grammar School.

Keep on in the same direction, noticing the street names attributed to famous men who had connections with the town – Chippendale and Turner, the famous landscape artist, who stayed at nearby Farnley Hall during his northern tours. Leave the houses behind and continue to rise until the entrance to Mount Pleasant farm is reached on the left of the road (GR208473). A signpost by a stile confirms the route diagonally across the field, leading to another stile in a short section of stone wall. Go over this, then continue with the hedge on your right, maintaining an almost straight course, passing close to Copmanroyd Farm buildings. Beyond these bear left towards a stile close to a telegraph pole. Cross this then turn right, passing between some modern houses to reach a main road.

Turn right and go up the hill then turn left and enter Roebuck Lane, alongside the public house. A damaged signpost to Clifton points the route along Roebuck Lane. Before reaching the last house turn right, passing through a gate, then go slightly left to another gate hidden in a depression. From there head diagonally left towards a stile just beyond the next enclosure. Beware of the dogs.

Maintain the same line, diagonally left, crossing three additional stiles before the course alters to accompany a section of fencing on the left. Follow the fence to an angle before bearing right, to cross the field, and pass through a gate by a water trough. Enter an enclosed lane and go on to the junction (GR193480). A right turn leads to the 'hidden' hamlet of Clifton, although the walk continues downhill to the left. As the lane descends bear right at the first junction and left at the next. When the enclosed section ends maintain the same general course, passing to the left of a copse, before entering East Wood. Once inside the wood swing left after half a dozen paces, continue downhill emerging on the main road close to some modern houses. This is Weston (GR185471).

Turn left along the road and go on for a good mile, until Ashfield House, a training centre for Leeds brewers Tetley's, is on the right. Here cross the road and enter the lane which leads to the Wharfedale Farmers' Market and Otley bridge, which is crossed to re-enter the town.

Other Dalesman titles for walkers

Walks Around Series: Peak District

BAKEWELL Martin Smith £1.99
BUXTON Andrew McCloy £1.99
CASTLETON John Gillham £1.99
MATLOCK Martin Smith £1.99

Walks Around Series: Lake District

AMBLESIDE Tom Bowker £1.99
HAWKSHEAD Mary Welsh £1.99
KESWICK Dawn Gibson £1.99
WINDERMERE Robert Gambles £1.99

Pub Walks Series

LAKE DISTRICT Terry Marsh 5.99
NORTH YORK MOORS & COAST Richard Musgrave £5.99
PEAK DISTRICT John Morrison £5.99
YORKSHIRE DALES Richard Musgrave £5.95

Walking and Trail Guides

NORTH PENNINES Alan Hall 4.99
WHITE PEAK Martin Smith £4.99
CLEVELAND WAY Martin Collins £4.99
SOUTH PENNINES John Gillham £4.99
DARK PEAK John Gillham £4.99
PENNINE WAY Terry Marsh £4.99
LAKE DISTRICT vol 1 £4.99
LAKE DISTRICT vol £4.99

Safety for Walkers

MOUNTAIN SAFETY Kevin Walker £4.99
MAP READING Robert Matkin 3.50

Available from all good bookshops.
In case of difficulty contact Dalesman Publishing Company, Clapham
Via Lancaster LA2 8EB 015242 51225